The New
Family Home

The New Family Home

CREATING THE PERFECT HOME for TODAY AND TOMORROW

Jim Tolpin
with Mary Lathrop

The Taunton Press

PUBLISHER: JIM CHILDS

ACQUISITIONS EDITOR: STEVE CULPEPPER

EDITOR: PETER CHAPMAN

ASSISTANT EDITOR: CAROL KASPER

ART DIRECTOR: PAULA SCHLOSSER

DESIGNER: TOMEK LAMPRECHT

PHOTOGRAPHER: DAVID LIVINGSTON, except where noted

ILLUSTRATOR: JACQUES ROCH

BOOKS & VIDEOS

for fellow enthusiasts

Printed in Singapore

10 9 8 7 6 5 4 3 2 1

The Taunton Press, Inc.,

63 South Main Street,

PO Box 5506,

Newtown, CT 06470-5506

e-mail: tp@taunton.com

Distributed by Publishers Group West

Library of Congress Cataloging-in-Publication Data
Tolpin, Jim, 1947-
The new family home : creating the perfect home for today and tomorrow / Jim Tolpin with Mary Lathrop.
p. cm.
ISBN 1-56158-354-5
1. Housing, Single family—United States. 2. Architecture, Domestic—United States.
3. Architecture, Modern—20th century—United States. I. Lathrop, Mary. II. Title.
NA7208.T65   2000   99-052583
728'.37—dc21   CIP

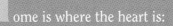ome is where the heart is:

I dedicate this book to my family.

Acknowledgments

I'd first like to acknowledge Mary Lathrop, a feature writer and playwright who joined me in the writing of this book. Her uncanny ability to ask the right questions gave voice to the 24 families whose homes are featured in this book. Her husband, George Lathrop, willing to listen to all we wrote, offered many useful suggestions.

In the development stage, my wife Catherine and friends Michele Bruns, Francis Natali, David Hagerman, and Peter Wilcox suggested insightful ways to get at the heart of just what constitutes a good family home. Architects Jim Sterling, Duo Dickinson, and James McNeely also offered valuable suggestions and productive leads to new family homes. Woodworker Gary Rogowski, architectural critic Randy Gragg of *The Oregonian,* Kingsley Hammett and Jerry Lou Hammett of *Designer/Builder* magazine, editor Leslie Clagett of *Today's Homeowner,* Susan Balcom of the *Vancouver Sun,* and Nancy Fishman in the Portland office of Zimmer Gunsul Frasca Architects all gave me leads to homes and their designers.

I'd like to give special thanks to architectural photographer David Livingston, whose images truly bring the idea of *The New Family Home* to life. Thanks also to David's mother, Ruth, for her delightful company on the photo shoots. At The Taunton Press, Jim Childs, Steve Culpepper, Peter Chapman, Paula Schlosser, Carol Kasper, Ellen Williams, and Tomek Lamprecht are due much appreciation for their ideas and efforts in the development and production of this book.

Of course, this book would not exist at all without the architects whose projects appear on these pages, nor without the families who hired and worked with them. These people graciously opened their homes and hearts to me, sharing with us all the dreams, hopes, and ultimate reality of their own vision of *The New Family Home.*

con tents

Introduction   1

THE FAMILY HOME   3

A PORTFOLIO OF NEW FAMILY HOMES   18

A Bungalow Built for Change   20
WASHINGTON

A Garden Home in the Heart of the City   28
CALIFORNIA

Texas Family Farmhouse   36
TEXAS

At Home in the Minnesota Pines   44
MINNESOTA

Starting Small, Dreaming Big   52
CALIFORNIA

Home for the Weekend   58
BRITISH COLUMBIA, CANADA

By the Beautiful Sea   68
CALIFORNIA

Family Dream Home   76
MASSACHUSETTS

A Home for the Generations   86
SOUTH CAROLINA

At Home on the Hill   94
MASSACHUSETTS

Timeless Beauty for a Modern Family   102
CALIFORNIA

Life on the River   110
MINNESOTA

At Play in Santa Barbara   118
CALIFORNIA

Northwoods Formal   126
MINNESOTA

Full Bloom in the Desert   134
NEW MEXICO

A Tale of Two Families   142
CONNECTICUT

Fly Away Home   150
WASHINGTON

The Many Lives of a Four-Flat   158
ILLINOIS

The New Family Farmhouse   166
CALIFORNIA

The Weekend Family Home   174
NEW YORK STATE

Blue Heron Ranch   182
CALIFORNIA

Bungalow by the Bay   190
WASHINGTON

A Scandinavian Farmhouse in
              the Pacific Northwest   198
WASHINGTON

The Maine House   206
MAINE

Architects and Designers   214

Introduction

A generation ago, "family" meant Mom, Dad, 2.3 kids, and a dog named Rover. Family homes were either nondescript ranches or neocolonial boxes. Not any more. The cookie-cutter tract houses of the 1950s and '60s are simply inadequate to meet the needs of modern families. Today, the people next door are telecommuting in their state-of-the-art home office. Their neighbors are homeschooling their young children. Down the block, a couple is planning a remodel now that the kids are grown and gone. Our houses must work harder than ever before.

As the pace of modern life grows more hectic, integrated kitchen/dining/living spaces allow families to spend precious at-home time together. Kid-friendly designs keep our children comfortable, happy—and safe—at home. Our electronic entertainment is relegated to media rooms or alcoves to help minimize its intrusion. Layouts are flexible so that rooms can adapt to different uses over time as the needs of family members change. And the inclusion of well-conceived home offices allows parents to integrate their work lives into the life of the family.

The 24 homes presented in *The New Family Home* all have stories to tell, and they tell them exceptionally well. These are all homes where the walls *do* talk—they speak of the time, energy, thought, and emotional investment that went into their creation. These houses demonstrate that the give and take of planning a new family home can actually bring our families closer together as we discover which spaces best serve our needs, what lessons we want to teach our children, and how we will live our lives.

The Family Home

After 30 years of marriage, two children, and a professional lifetime spent building their Vancouver business, Ernest and Grace Collins needed something more. They'd bought a little land in a small mountain valley three hours to the north, with plans for a weekend getaway. But as the plans took shape, they realized that a part-time home wasn't the solution. What they wanted was a full-time home, a one-of-a-kind place designed just for them, which would work hard for the whole family.

The Collins started from scratch to design and build a new type of house, a comfortable, safe haven for themselves and their kids, with a large, versatile open space to encourage togetherness but with enough private space for personal time alone. It would be a home where they could be with their children yet maintain their professional lives—a place where they could work, but also rest and relax. Above all, it would be a home that worked for the family through all the changes to come.

In a few years, their daughter will be in college and Vancouver will be in the past, as the home becomes the full-time base for their business. They still run their offices in Vancouver, but they alternate weeks in the city overseeing business while the other works out of their home office, minds their high school-age daughter (their son is in college), and keeps the home fires burning. The Collins live in a *New Family Home*.

Things Aren't What They Used to Be

The New Family Home that works for Ernest and Grace Collins wouldn't work for some other families. And it definitely wouldn't have worked for their parents. Things just aren't what they used to be.

The statistical changes over the past 50 years are staggering. More than one-quarter of Americans are single parents. Four million children live with their grandparents. Nearly one-third of the labor force works from home 35 hours a week or more. And everybody works longer hours, on and off the job. Even our children are caught up in a whirlwind of activ-

ities, with packed schedules after school and on weekends. All the while, new technologies keep transforming the way we work, communicate, learn, and entertain ourselves.

Within our own lifetimes, the definition of family has become very broad. Of course, the *Leave It To Beaver* families that defined an earlier generation are still around, but in every town, and on every street, traditional families live next door to step-families, single-parent families, blended families, extended families, empty-nesters, and multi-generation families.

Even traditional families change. And as they do, their homes change too—that's the key to *The New Family Home*. The traditional collection of formal living room and dining room, kitchen, and three bedrooms worked fine when mom stayed put and dad brought home the bacon. But a lot of people don't live like that anymore. In a brick-and-mortar way, our homes have had to respond to fundamental changes in how we work, rest, and play. Homes have to do more. They still accommodate all the stuff we accumulate, but they also have to make space

for computers, video equipment, audio systems, and, increasingly, space for working at home. *The New Family Home* is all things to all members of the family.

This Place Called Home

What Ernest and Grace accomplished is being realized all across the country, in all kinds and sizes of homes, for all kinds and sizes of families. Although these houses are often radically different, a handful of trends guides them all.

The most important of these trends is the desire to create a very personal home, to make rooms and spaces specifically for an individual family. Architect Brian Cearnal built such a place for his family in southern California. In his opinion, "The trick is to create a home that allows you to live the way you really want to live, not just how you think you ought to live."

Left **The traditional idea of rooms for separate activities—be it cooking, eating, or watching TV— has been replaced in the New Family Home by open, communal areas that encourage family members to spend time together.**

Opposite, top **Homes of an earlier generation tended to isolate family members from one another. Kitchens were often sterile, almost laboratory-like cubicles closed off from the dining and living areas. (Photo courtesy FPG International LLC)**

Opposite, bottom **In the 1950s home, television was invariably the focal point of the living room. In the New Family Home, television and other media entertainments are often relegated to a separate room or alcove where they won't dominate family life. (Photo courtesy Archive Photos/Lambert)**

So *out* is excess square footage, oversized bedrooms, bathrooms for every member of the family, walled-off dining room and living room—all within a facade scaled to dwarf the neighbor's house. *In* is the home that works from corner to corner, with a design that gets used and tested every day, that is carefully designed inwardly, yet just as carefully fitted to its site.

Something else significant keeps appearing in *The New Family Home*, a sense that home is a place to bring everyone together, not to send them off to their rooms. Call it nostalgia for simpler times, when a family at home was a family together. Call it family values. Whatever spin gets put on it, *The New Family Home* strives to be the most important place to everybody in the family. But to be such a place, it must really work for the people who call it home. Independent-minded teenagers have room to be with friends—not in a soundproof vault, but in a space that's just far enough away so others aren't disturbed. Young children have room to play and to

safely watch the world around them. And though the family might well be able to afford more room, brother often bunks with brother, sister with sister. It seems that sharing space is a good exercise for learning to share more meaningful things.

You'll also find a place to work in *The New Family Home*, offices eased into the design so that making a living from home is an attractive option that allows parents to integrate work life with home life. Not only are home work spaces assimilated seamlessly into the home, but television, video games, and music are all fitted into places where whoever wants to enjoy them can, but without everybody else having to listen.

Working at home is a major trend, and in a family home it's critical that the office ties in with both the building and the lifestyle. In some of these homes, you'll see offices that were deliberately set in the middle of everything, where one parent or another can earn a living and at the same time keep up with what the kids are doing. In other homes, offices are in separate structures, altogether removed from the family routine but still close by. And in some cases, work areas remain in the home but are kept apart, isolated from the sound and traffic.

Ultimately, these homes reflect not only the people who live in them now, but who they will be years down the road. American families typically move about every five years. Because pulling up roots, switching jobs, changing schools, leaving family and friends behind takes its toll, many families aspire to something more permanent. People who live in a *New Family Home* are staying put in a place where they can grow old and live comfortably, where their children can grow up, move out into the world, and return to visit with their own children.

As more Americans find ways to earn a living at home, the home office—from a built-in desk set into a stairway alcove to an office tower annex—is increasingly becoming a must-have feature of the New Family Home.

These houses look into the future and anticipate change. Rooms that serve one function today, serve a different function tomorrow. In a Seattle suburb, the main-floor guest suite in Johan and Robin Luchsinger's home is always open for visiting grandparents. Ten years from now when their son is a teenager, the guest room will become his room—a private space on a separate floor from his parents. Once their son has moved away, the room might next serve as a home office or media room. And, ultimately, the space will assume yet another life when Johan and Robin reach the age when they'd rather not climb the stairs and so turn the suite into their own bedroom.

Chicago architect Scott Rappe noticed this trend: "Until recently, people bought properties thinking that they'd keep them a short time and then turn them over. But one way of holding onto the value is to stay put and build on the house you already have." This runs counter to the idea that "success" means trading up through a succession of increasingly big homes, then cashing in and retiring to a sunny condo in some place warmer.

Making a Mark on the Family Home

Just as there's no one definition of what it means to be a family, there's no one style unique to *The New Family Home*. The homes you'll see inside were all built or remodeled in the past 10 years, and as much as they show the amazing diversity of the family, they also showcase the remarkable variety of residential architecture.

Houses range from traditional to ultramodern, from compact to imposing. Our *New Family Homes* include a renovated "four-flat" in Chicago, a rambling wine-country farmhouse, a storybook starter home in California, a stylish contemporary in upstate New York, an Arts and Crafts–style bungalow in suburban Seattle, a colorful home in the New Mexican desert. Like all of our families, each of our homes is a unique creation.

The New Family Home is built for change, with rooms that can assume different functions as family needs change. A guest room that today provides a private and serene space for visitors might one day serve as a bedroom for a teenager, a home office, a den, or a master bedroom for aging parents.

Families here contributed more than just money toward the creation of their homes. Without exception, the homeowners thought long and hard about what and where they wanted their home to be. They've invested their own time and energy in the design—put serious effort into getting a house that's just right for their family, even if it takes years to pull it all together.

A family in the Pacific Northwest built a pair of river-rock columns on either side of the front porch and set the mortar with pieces of colored glass they found on their property to help make the place really theirs. Inside, they created rooms that work for just the family they are today but that can change to reflect who they will be in a decade—or two. Another family set their own history into the very structure of the house. They placed a steel time capsule (full of personal notes, photos, and plans that document the creation of their home) in one of the columns that separate the sitting and dining rooms. A family in downtown San Francisco keeps chickens in the

Whether a renovated row house in the city, a cottage bungalow in a small town, a contemporary villa on a hill, or a postmodern adobe in the desert, the New Family Home is a unique, yet practical expression of the family it was created for. (Photo at far right by Kirk Gittings)

backyard. They call their home the "Lazy-Egg Ranch." Ernest and Grace Collins literally put their brand on their new home, which they dubbed "Morning Star." Using hand-forged iron star brands, they and their neighbors christened the home by burning stars into the deck and its furniture.

A strong sense of place also fills these *New Family Homes*. Whether they're in a Minnesota pine forest, by the sea, or in an urban neighborhood, families are giving a lot of thought to where they want to live. Through landscape, views, light—or by staying true to local building traditions—these homes relate to the land as well as to the family.

Kids at the Center

For most parents, the world of the family revolves around the kids. They try our patience, but we love them. And we really want them to feel at home when they're at home. So how do we make a house so welcoming that even teenagers want to spend time at home? Give them a

place they can take over. When they're off to college, the room becomes something else.

Lots of thought goes into all the rooms for kids in *The New Family Home*. Inside, we'll see how parents took pains to rethink where these rooms should be. For instance, the location of kids' rooms relative to the master bedroom often depends on children's ages. Putting a small child's room close to the master suite keeps very young children feeling safe at night. As kids approach their teen years, parents and children are comfortable with more separate sleeping arrangements. When there are three children or more—even when the children are still rel-

A girl's bedroom features a floor-to-ceiling mirror with a dance barre. Stackable plastic bins provide convenient storage for a stuffed animal collection. A second bed accommodates overnight visits from siblings or guests.

atively young—separating their rooms from the parents' bedroom can work just fine. Huddle several children together in their own wing, and they rest easy in each other's company.

In homes where brothers or sisters share bedrooms, some families are including a common play area where they have to work at sharing. A family in the Midwest created tiny bedrooms for their children to make it more likely that the kids will play together instead of hunkering down in their rooms.

There's no rule that says kids have to have their own bedrooms. In fact, lessons in civility and consideration start at an early age when children share bedrooms.

Places where kids can play are common in *The New Family Home.* Big toys, loud games, wild kids can all happen indoors, if the house was planned that way. With kid chaos confined, the children's bedrooms can be peaceful hideaways for sleeping and reading. A play space doesn't even have to be a room. One family carved a little play space out of a wide stair landing—halfway between two worlds. Another family put in an extra-wide hallway that doubles as a play area.

And then there's something known as a "kid corridor," which is just a path well beaten by the children. If it is planned just right, a typical kid corridor might join the backyard swing set with the mudroom, a family bathroom, the playroom, and the children's bedrooms in a big circuit. At the hub of this circuit would be the kitchen/family room, where a grown-up can stay out of the way but maintain control.

For older kids and teenagers, a space set apart from the center of the house gives privacy and a sense of independence. One family gave the older kids a huge chunk of their basement, including a walk-out, which pretty much sets them up in an autonomous apartment (a far cry from the traditional family room where teens could get together only if mom was on the other side of the door). They've got a television and stereo, of course, but they've also got a kitchenette with a dormitory refrigerator and microwave. Real independence, but within earshot of the open central stairwell.

Putting Television in Its Place

Getting the television out of the center of the house and into a place like these basement quarters allows teenagers to turn up the volume without disturbing the rest of the house, another departure from the recent past. A real selling point in many postwar suburban homes was a built-in TV set that served as the evening entertainment for the whole family. Of course, television still holds hostage much of the American family's time—as do video games, stereos, and the Internet. But television sets almost never make an appearance in living rooms these days and are, in fact, becoming increasingly rare even in family rooms.

To combat the lure of easy, passive entertainment, *The New Family Home* puts our gadgets in their place. Separate rooms or discrete alcoves make sure that all of these distractions aren't right in the center of things. Only the person actually using them has to see and hear them. Like teenagers.

Above **A room set apart from the center of the house gives teenagers some privacy and a sense of independence.**

Opposite, top and bottom **A key feature of many New Family Homes is the large, central, open space that integrates cooking, dining, and living activities. Subtly defined areas within the space delineate separate functions without cutting them off from one another.**

All Things to All People

Inside *The New Family Home* you'll sense a longing for times when families spent more time together, when the world outside was less gray, more black-and-white, and the pace was slower. *The New Family Home* is the center of this universe, a place for simple, content family life. Because the pace of life is fast and time is short, it makes sense that we pull the family together and turn toward home.

How can the design of a home help bring a family together? Well, instead of separate rooms for separate goings-on (meals, music, Monopoly), communal areas encourage the family to share their time at home. Call it a great room, a living hall, a great hall, or whatever, this open space allows for feelings of closeness and a sense of

connection—where no one is isolated from the flow of family life—unless they choose to be.

Space, rather than walls, separates one activity from another while keeping parents and kids close enough. Certain activities, like music and games, might be settled into alcoves or semi-enclosed spaces within the big room. Changes in ceiling height, wall finishes, and flooring all help define its many uses. A lot goes on here, but the family room can hold it all.

This family room mixes kitchen, dining, and living rooms, which usually means that it's the largest, most open area in the house. And it's a prominent feature of more than half the homes in the book. In many families, this room has supplanted the traditional living room as a place to entertain. Typically, it's situated at the rear of the home, away from the street and the outside world, where family and friends are drawn into the world of a family.

Above, left **A master bedroom, awash in the warm glow of the morning sun, offers a retreat from the joyful chaos of family life—at least until the kids wake up.**

Above, right **A funky tire swing and tree fort are the perfect complements to a beautiful, thoughtfully designed New Family Home, a place created to make a family feel perfectly at home.**

The key to success in these homes is balance: between places set aside for everybody, and places of privacy and calm. For instance, the master suite has become much larger—in many cases, it's one of the most luxurious rooms in the house. In *The New Family Home,* the master suite often serves two purposes: it's a retreat for the home-owners and a mini-family room. Bay Area architect Fu Tung Cheng designed just such a place for a family of six. Downstairs, the two boys share one room and their two sisters share another. On the second floor, the parents can luxuriate in a large suite that includes a small drawing room. In this most private area of the house, a cozy sitting area in front of a fireplace or a spa-like master bathroom often becomes a spot for the family to gather for a few moments, often in the evening.

Bringing It All Back Home

A flood of trends and changes in family life has made us rethink the way we design, build, and use the home. At the heart of *The New Family Home,* however, is a hunger for stability. Although working families spend less time at home than they ever did, they are spending more money and time on their homes and comforts, figuring out what they need, crafting sanctuaries apart from the rush.

These *New Family Homes* are designed to respond to the needs of the family, not to some dated fiction of what we were. These are individual, deeply personal designs that are 180-degrees from the faceless ranches and neocolonial boxes that many of us grew up in. There is less concern with square footage, oversized bedrooms, a bathroom for every family member, and resale value, and more attention to what real families really want. There is care and planning. There is family. There is home.

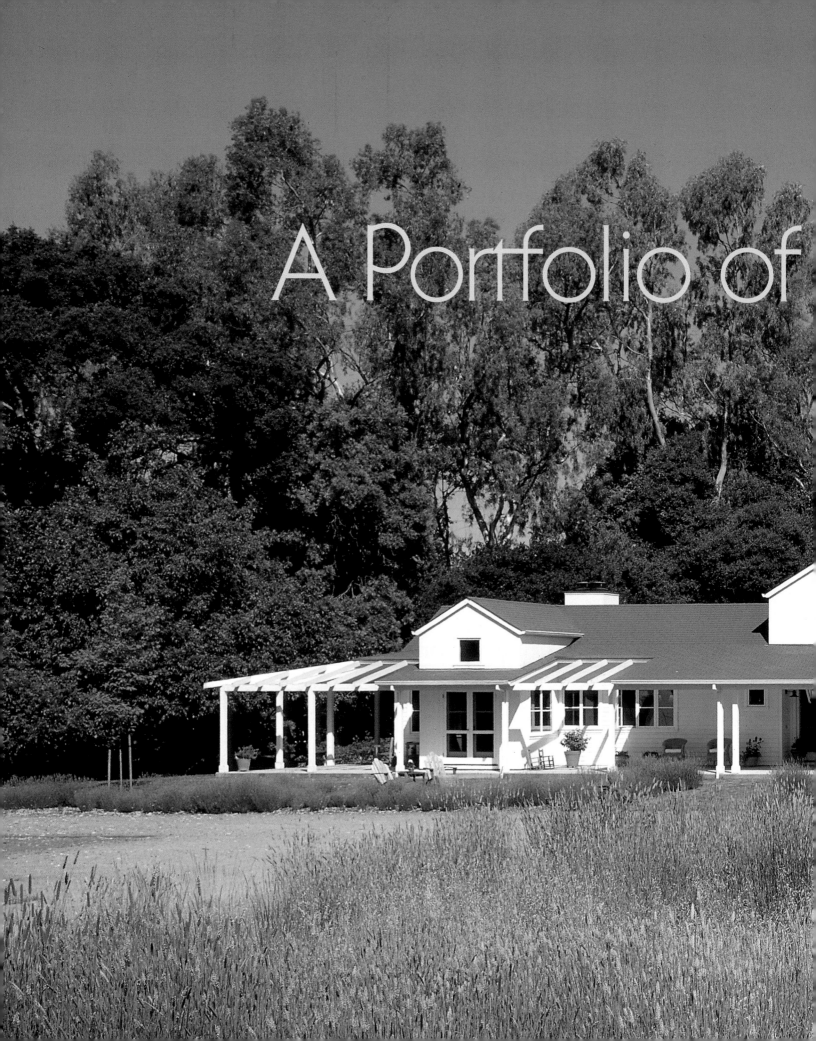

A Portfolio of

New
Family Homes

From the moment that architect Johan Luchsinger and his interior designer wife Robin learned they were expecting a baby, they realized that the days in their tiny, 1,200-sq.-ft. classic Seattle bungalow were numbered. Their goal was to take what they loved best about their 1923 in-city cottage, combine it with features more in keeping with their new lifestyle as parents, expand it all to a comfortable size in which to raise a growing son, and build the home of their dreams on a beautiful piece of land that they could cherish and preserve for the future.

A Bungalow
Built for Change

Like many people building family homes today, Johan and Robin were looking for ideas that would serve them for the long term. They wanted a home in which they could raise their family and grow old together, a place that they might someday hand down to the next generation. The house they envisioned was to be a thoughtfully constructed bungalow that had comfortably sized spaces and room for extended visits from grandparents. Equally important, the home would be adaptable to meet the family's needs as those needs changed over time.

Eventually, the Luchsingers found a two-third-acre lot with groves of maples and alders and several old-growth fir trees. The quiet woodiness of the site lent itself well to the Arts and Crafts-style lodge that they wanted to build. The home's exterior is an unusual choice for its suburban location, featuring the rustic appeal of an earlier era, with cedar shingles, divided-light casement windows, and deep roof overhangs. A separate garage, set

Above **The vaulted ceiling creates a feeling of spaciousness in the first-floor guest bedroom. The exposed ridge beam reveals the structure of the house, a typical Arts and Crafts detail.**

Right **This home features river-rock columns supporting a traditional front porch, true divided-light windows, and cedar-shake siding—all elements of the classic Arts and Crafts–style urban bungalow re-created here in a new Seattle suburb.**

Opposite *Transom windows, generous side lights, and a skylight illuminate the gracious entry hall, which leads directly to the family room and kitchen beyond. The Craftsman-style oak balustrade was custom designed by the owners.*

Right *Tucked in groves of alder, maple, and fir, the home has been sited to preserve as many trees as possible. The separate carriage house–style garage—an unusual choice for the suburbs—enhances the traditional bungalow ambiance.*

well apart from the house, has the appearance of an old-fashioned carriage house. The overall look and feel is of a family compound.

Room to Grow

One of the hallmarks of the new family home is that it's built with an eye to the future. High on Robin and Johan's list of priorities, for example, was a third bedroom. It was a room they needed right away so that visiting grandparents could spend lots of time with their young grandson. They gave the space a private bathroom and easy access on the first floor, away from the two second-floor family bedrooms. A French door leads directly outside, giving the guest quarters a feeling of autonomy.

A decade from now when the Luchsingers' son is a teenager, the guest room might very well become his room, which will allow him a certain amount of independence and give Robin and Johan added privacy and acoustic separation. Once their son is grown and has moved away, this room might next become a home office or a quiet den. Further down the road, this same space could easily be transformed into a first-floor master bedroom, with the second-floor family bedrooms and bathroom closed off and reserved as guest quarters for when their grown son visits with children of his own.

Another example of flexible room design is just inside the door to the Luchsingers' master suite upstairs. While they had originally planned to have a small master bathroom, once the house was framed in Johan and Robin decided that the space could better serve as a compact home office for Robin. Robin especially likes having a place to work just across the hallway from her son's bedroom—while he's playing, she is nearby in case he needs anything.

This is a design strategy that works especially well when there are young children in the home; the close proximity to parents enhances the sense of security for the children, which in turn minimizes interruptions. In the future, the mini-office space could be used as an "insomnia" room or even a second walk-in closet for the master bedroom. And Johan and Robin never have to regret their decision to leave out the master bathroom—if they ever change their minds, the plumbing is already installed inside the walls.

Keeping it Green

The Luchsingers made a conscious effort to address green architecture, in keeping with their feelings of stewardship for their property. The house and garage were both sited to avoid removing trees, and the house is oriented for maximum solar gain. Recycled timbers (some salvaged from an old church) helped keep construction costs in line while providing the Luchsingers with high-quality materials.

Above **Both upstairs bedrooms feature large, walk-in closets. French-style, casement windows are set high on the wall to bring in natural light and fresh air without compromising privacy.**

Opposite **This pleasant, well-lit eating nook off the kitchen is a good place for a late-morning cup of coffee, an after-school snack, or an intimate, informal family supper. Easy access to the outside deck is through French doors, which provide additional light and ventilation.**

T he owners of this home had been living comfortably in their San Francisco townhouse for a number of years, but the arrival of their first child made them realize that, perhaps, they didn't have quite enough space. The arrival of child number two a few years later confirmed their suspicions. The couple loved their neighborhood, loved their urban lifestyle, and wanted to share the pleasures of the city with their children as they grew. If they were going to move to a larger house, it would have to be in the city, not out in the suburbs. But everything they could afford to buy in San Francisco needed extensive upgrading, remodeling,

A Garden Home in the Heart of the City

or both. And besides, they loved their own little home and their beautiful private garden. Ultimately, the decision to stay where they were and build onto what they already had was easy.

The couple came to Bobbie-Sue Hood, an architect well known for her work restoring and remodeling the grand old Victorians of San Francisco. The homeowners needed more living space and at least one more bedroom, and they were especially concerned about preserving as much of their beloved garden as possible. In addition to the expansion, they hoped to remodel their kitchen and transform a first-floor bedroom into an acoustically isolated home office.

Bobbie-Sue suggested a two-story addition that would feature a large solarium-style living room with a spacious porch on the first floor to take maximum advantage of the garden setting, a rec room for the kids in the basement, and a large master bedroom and bath-

Above **The curve of the front porch and the arch above the gable soften the facade of this San Francisco townhouse. Grapevines on the trellis shade the porch and filter the light of the conservatory great room.**

Opposite **An ancient cherry tree frames the front entrance. According to the principles of Feng Shui, the bright red front door will frighten away evil spirits.**

children grow from infancy through adolescence, an ever-changing set of demands is placed on family homes. Spaces that can adapt to meet those changing needs are the hallmark of a good design. For these homeowners, the quiet library could better serve their family as a media room, a space used primarily for kid-related activities. This is where the children watch television, play computer games, set up their toys, and hang out with their friends. Pocket doors can be closed to provide privacy and sound isolation.

When the homeowners first came to Bobbie-Sue, they asked her to give them two additional bedrooms. Bobbie-Sue convinced them that they would be happier in the long run with a single, spacious master bedroom instead. The master bedroom features a large skylight, a bird's-eye view of the garden, and a small private deck. The owners are glad they followed Bobbie-Sue's advice. Out-of-town company is put up in the media room downstairs, which helps to preserve the family's privacy upstairs. The two children's bedrooms open onto a shared back hallway that leads to an additional family bathroom. Rather than being wasted space, this carpeted hallway helps isolate bathroom noise and doubles as a favorite play area.

The first-floor home office at the back of the house is accessed through the kitchen and by an exterior door that opens to the back of the property. It's a professional office space that's used full time by one of the homeowners. Because this space is a place of business, acoustic isolation was a high priority. When they were babies, the children often came along to work, where a playpen was set up for their use. Now that they are older, they frequently play close by in the media room. If the family feels the need for more living space in the future, the business might be moved out of the home. The same acoustic isolation and sense of separation that make this a successful home office are features that would make it a good choice as a teen retreat as well.

Above **Set above the conservatory great room, the master bedroom has a view over the garden to the cityscape beyond. A large skylight directly over the bed brings in natural light by day and a view of the night sky after the sun goes down.**

Opposite **Book-filled shelves line the walls of the media room. Painting bookshelves to match the walls lessens their visual imposition, especially important in a small space.**

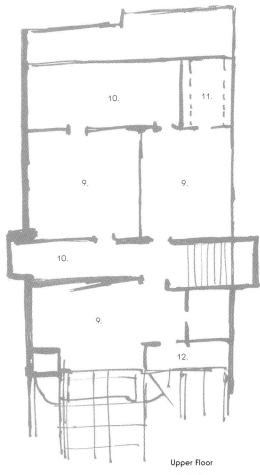

Upper Floor

9. Bedroom
10. Bath
11. Walk-in Closet
12. Deck

Left *The porch extends the living space all the way into the garden and is a favorite spot for meals. The deep rafters supporting the trellis cast shadows until the grapevines can create a full canopy of their own.*

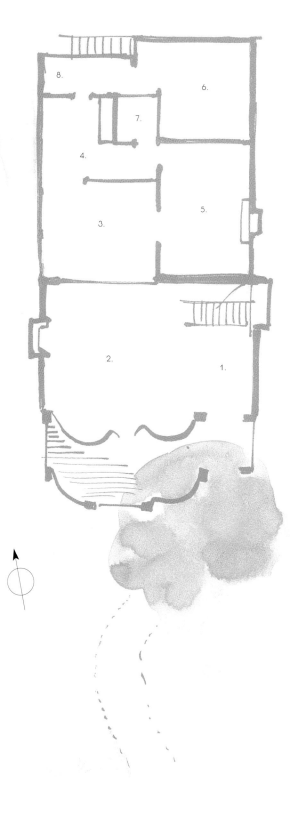

Main Floor

1. Entry
2. Great Hall
3. Dining Room
4. Kitchen
5. Media Room
6. Home Office
7. Bath
8. Powder Room

a century of transformation

This home in San Francisco has been through many incarnations. Built in 1904 as a small, four-room cottage, it survived the 1906 earthquake and escaped the great fire that destroyed nearly all of the buildings in the area. According to historical records, the cottage was used as an Army field hospital to tend the injured in the fire's aftermath—the homeowners have unearthed several old medicine bottles and U.S. military crockery shards while digging in their garden over the years.

Rooms in the original structure were remodeled in the 1950s, and a second story was added in the 1970s. When the homeowners completed the latest addition in the early 1990s, they had quadrupled the space of the original four-room cottage. And during the remodel, they uncovered copies of 1904 San Francisco newspapers that were hidden inside the walls—insulation material used in the original construction.

When Deborah and Nick Denner got married, their ready-made family included her two daughters and his son from previous marriages, and before long they were joined by a baby daughter of their own. But the Denner family will disagree if you call them a "blended" family. "We're more of a 'blendered' family. We've worked hard to transform his, hers, and theirs into all ours," explains Debbie Denner. For the Denners, an important part of growing together as a whole family was the creation of the Texas ranch-style home they built on five acres in the hill country outside Austin.

Texas Family Farmhouse

The Denners had a lot of priorities to sort out as they began planning their new house. Foremost, the home needed to address the current and changing needs of their growing children. Since this home was being built for the long term, they also needed to consider what would be best for the two of them later on in life when the children were grown and gone. Whenever and wherever possible, they wanted to make sure the house was built using sustainable and green building techniques. By addressing all of these needs, they hoped to have a positive effect on their family, their environment, and the land itself.

A Pattern for Living

Debbie and Nick found an enthusiastic partner for their project in architect Ken Foster. Ken gave the Denners a copy of *A Pattern Language* by Christopher Alexander to read and study. In the book, Alexander talks about the 253 elements in a built environment that people gravitate to naturally. For example, people are drawn to a fire, so it's logical to put a fireplace in a central location. The

Above **This low-profile, naturally finished house lives lightly on the land and in harmony with it. The paths are an integral part of the landscaping, leading all around the house and to the homeowner's office and the garage. (Photo by Steve Culpepper)**

Opposite **The Southwestern-style fireplace links this Texas home to its historical roots. Window seats are cozy alcoves, intimate spaces within the larger great room. The wooden ceiling is indirectly lit for a feeling of warmth and spaciousness.**

Left *Stair-step bookshelves—a clever and efficient use of space—lead to the children's play loft. Copper pipes serve as handrails. The piano alcove opens off the dining room.*

Below *The central family gathering area is a great room with an open kitchen at its core. Light fills the space, and air moves freely in this reinterpretation of an old-style Texas farmhouse.*

Denners used Alexander's book to help make decisions about room layout, building details, floor materials, and window and furniture placement.

The home was created around the idea that there should be places for the whole family to gather together, cozy nooks where two or three family members would be comfortable, and spaces for everyone to maintain their privacy and independence. Ultimately, Nick and Debbie picked 65 of Alexander's elements to include in their new home. From the positioning of windows to the pool of light that illuminates the dining table, Alexander's influence is seen and felt in every room of the house.

The largest public space is an integrated living room, dining room, and kitchen. In this variation on the great room, the open, airy kitchen is at the center, very much the heart of the home. The living room's fireplace is positioned in a corner and flanked by built-in window seats, cozy spots for quiet conversation or afternoon daydreaming. A loft above the dining area lowers the ceiling height for a more intimate feeling and is a favorite play area for the Denner kids. A piano alcove off the dining room provides another small, intimate space that is still connected to the larger great room.

Sleeping Arrangements

Placing parents' and children's bedrooms in close proximity is a strategy that helps enhance everyone's sense of security. However, when children are older or when there are three or more children to keep each other company, isolation from the parents' bedroom is not as significant an issue. While many families choose to cluster bedrooms in a single location, Debbie and Nick wanted a private space of their own, removed from the hubbub of children's activities. At the Denner house, the four children have their own bedroom wing, which is entered through a shared playroom.

"The kids really like having this separate space to entertain their friends," comments Debbie. Glass doors can be closed to enhance the children's sense of privacy while allowing parents to keep a

Above **The playroom isn't all play—the laundry facilities are tucked behind louvered doors in the children's wing. The homeowners requested this placement to encourage their children to be responsible for their own laundry.**

Right **The playroom is a foyer to the children's bedrooms. French doors in the foreground close for privacy when friends are visiting but allow parents to keep an eye on the action.**

discrete eye on activities. Bedrooms for the children are purposely small to encourage use of the communal parts of the house.

The master suite is situated away from the children's wing on the opposite side of the central public rooms. This arrangement works well—the children know their parents are available if they need them, and Nick and Debbie like the feeling of having their own private retreat at the end of the day. The Denners can foresee a time in the future when the children's wing can be closed off from the rest of the house, to be opened for visits from children and grandchildren.

Catching the Rain

Achieving balance for spaces and systems was important in every aspect of this project. Materials were carefully chosen. Aware that many interior building materials outgas toxins, the Denners consciously chose natural fiber carpeting, water-based lacquers, and other nontoxic/low-toxic alternatives for the interior of the house. "For the Denners, it was especially important to create an environment for their family that reflected the wholeness they strive to achieve in their own lives," reflects Ken Foster.

Just off the master suite is a large open-air pavilion, much used by every member of the family. The walkways and paths that circle the house all lead to it quite naturally. Used as a place for playing, eating, relaxing, and entertaining, this outdoor room makes the Denner home act and feel bigger than it actually is. The pavilion serves another purpose, as well—it is the top of the 26,000-gallon cistern that provides the Denner family with all of their household water. The household depends entirely on rainwater catchment, with the roofs of house, porches, office, and carport all serving as catchment areas.

Above **Separated from the children's wing, the master bedroom is the owners' private retreat at bedtime. During the day, it is often used by the children as a quiet place to catch a favorite television show.**

Opposite **A favorite hangout and a shady playground for children, this open-air pavilion tops the water cistern. The 26,000 gallons of captured rainwater keep the area pleasantly cool, even on the hottest days.**

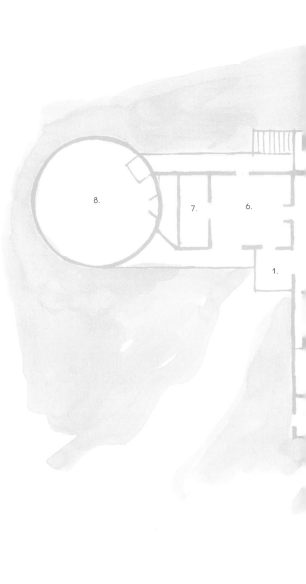

According to Nick, putting in the catchment system was one of the best decisions they made. "Out here in the Texas hill country, the water is very hard," he explains. "Our neighbors can drink only bottled water, for example. Our water is wonderful. Our oldest daughter's friends come out here to wash their hair. We do have a well used for some external watering, but even the plants don't really like it."

Left *A rustic bridge leads to the homeowner's office, a separate building nestled in a grove of trees.*

Main Floor

1. Entry
2. Living Room
3. Kitchen
4. Dining Nook
5. Piano Alcove
6. Master Bedroom
7. Master Bath
8. Pavilion
9. Playroom
10. Bedroom
11. Bath
12. Screen Porch

beating the heat

In addition to using the latest in green building techniques, the Denner house incorporates design ideas from traditional Texas architecture. Architect Ken Foster is especially in tune with the past through historic preservation work he has done for the Texas Department of Parks and Wildlife. "Before there was electricity or air conditioning, people had to build according to the climate. It's hot in Texas nine months out of the year, so it's a question of keeping a house cool," says Ken.

Traditional Texan houses were open in the middle to create a cross breeze. Called a "dog trot" in the old days, the open public rooms at the center of the Denner house function in much the same way. The house is set on an east-west axis to pick up the prevailing southern breeze, so every major room has windows on at least two sides. Not only does this allow for adequate ventilation, but the placement of windows also cuts down on glare and improves the quality of light.

Other old-time ideas adopted for beating the heat include using wide overhangs on all sides for shade, installing a vented cupola at the peak of the roof so that rising heat can escape, nestling the house between small groves of trees for added shade, and choosing light colors for the exterior that reflect the heat.

A richly appointed, beautifully landscaped estate home with an expansive green lawn, a swimming pool, and a tennis court. A custom-built log cabin for weekends at the lake. Herb Pilhofer and RoseMary Januschka had it all—but they weren't sure they wanted it anymore. Herb and RoseMary were starting to feel possessed by their possessions. Their time was being used up caring for their two houses, their belongings, and that enormous green lawn, when what they really wanted was to relax and enjoy life with their young children. When a pristine 20-acre parcel covered with dense pine forest became available, they grabbed it, ready to

At Home in the
Minnesota Pines

create a cozy family home under the trees. It was the perfect spot to simplify their lives and raise their family.

The Pilhofers asked architect Katherine Cartrette to design a home that would fit into the forest setting by incorporating a log-timber frame, a broad, sheltering roof, and lots of natural materials. The home was to have a Northwoods elegance, but with no formal rooms, no wasted space. There was to be work space for Herb, a professional musician and composer. Television, video, and computers were to be set away from the family's primary living area. The parents wanted the children close by while they were still young, but the home needed to provide the kids with adequate space and privacy when they became teenagers.

The new Pilhofer family home sits on a sunny knoll amid the fragrant pine forest. Essentially, it's a Craftsman-style lodge, but the

Above **Incorporating beloved family treasures into the design of a room is a dramatic and effective way to personalize a family home. Here, a carved German chest holds a place of honor in the great room.**

Opposite **Upper and lower decks bring the house right into the forest. Generous overhangs keep rain off the windows and protect the siding and the foundation. The outdoor fireplace creates an outdoor "room," a favorite spot for family and friends to gather.**

materials used in its construction set it apart. The post-and-beam construction is of natural logs, which were stripped of their bark and then varnished. The design blends elements of traditional Asian and Bavarian architecture with the building materials of the American frontier.

Home Work and Play

Families today typically ask architects to include some kind of home-office space in their new homes. Depending on the home-owners' needs, the office might be anything from a small desk alcove to professional office space in a completely separate structure. Herb had very specific needs for his home work space. In addition to requesting desk space for the fax and the computer, he required room to work at his grand piano and a small recording studio.

The home's lower (basement) level turned out to be the perfect location for a music studio. Floors and walls are of poured concrete, which provides excellent sound isolation. Careful planning and additional, well-chosen insulation materials in the interior walls and ceiling help ensure that the noise of family life on the main floor does not intrude into the studio below.

The Pilhofers asked Katherine to make a place for the television that was separate from the primary family living space. The media room is on the lower level adjacent to Herb's studio. When Herb is working during the day, the media room is off-limits to the kids, but in the evenings and on the weekends, the lower level becomes a spacious family room that is used and enjoyed by everyone. Comfortable furniture, windows that look out over the woods, a massive rock fireplace, and top-of-the-line audio and video equipment make this a great entertainment center.

The Pilhofers like the way this multi-use space functions, and the restrictions that Herb's work time puts on the kids' television time

Above *A shrine in the woods honors the family's heritage and roots. Typical of the small wayside chapels found in the Alps, this handcrafted shrine was a gift from husband to wife to mark the birth of their children.*

Left *The lower level is an open gallery of rooms. In the foreground, the home-owner's music studio is acoustically isolated from the living space upstairs. The media center is just beyond.*

actually improves the quality of everyone's daily activities. In addition, the same acoustic isolation that keeps things quiet down in the music studio prevents the noise of television and stereo equipment from filtering into the living room and master bedroom above.

A Casual Elegance

The main living space is open and informal, a great room that contains living, dining, and cooking space. Herb and RoseMary don't miss having formal rooms for entertaining. "We put out our beautiful china and crystal from Germany," explains RoseMary. "You can take a casual setting and make it very elegant."

The most striking features in the great room are the natural forms of the post-and-beam construction and the massive rock fireplace. Uprights with natural crooks support beams with natural arches. The rocks that face the fireplace are a cool contrast to the warmth of the wood. According to Katherine, old photos of a lodge at Yellowstone were the inspiration for the fireplace. The low pitch of the ceiling gives the large room a real coziness. "There was a lot of discussion about roof pitch," recalls Herb. "We definitely didn't want a high soaring ceiling. We wanted something with the proportions and charm of a European-style lodge."

Home Is Where the Hearth Is

This is a home of fireplaces, all of which share the soaring rock chimney. In addition to the main hearth in the great room and the fireplace in the media room downstairs, a third hearth is just outside on the patio. The Pilhofers use the outdoor hearth year-round, and the patio and deck that surround it are significant living spaces in the life of the family. In the summer, an outdoor fire lights up parties on the deck, and during the winter months, family and friends like to gather round the blazing outdoor hearth after a day of cross-country skiing and sledding. Outdoor living spaces that

Above *A row of kitchen cabinets faces out into the living space, fine furniture for the great room that also provides additional storage space for the kitchen.*

Opposite *The great room is an eclectic mixture of rustic and refined elements. Hand-peeled logs, natural stone, hardwood floors, oriental rugs, and leather furniture create a warm and personal family space.*

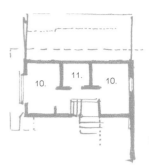

Upper Floor
10. Bedroom
11. Bath

Left **Built-ins make efficient use of space in the children's bedrooms. Trundle beds are the perfect solution for sleepovers. The view into the trees gives this space a treehouse feeling.**

Below **The current pool (the water moves, the swimmer doesn't) is much used by the children, who are both active in intramural swimming programs. It's a dog's life for the coach, a certified water retriever.**

are as carefully planned as the Pilhofers' outdoor hearth can have a huge impact on a family and the way they spend their time.

Small Rooms Are Room Enough

RoseMary and Herb gave much thought to the size and placement of the family bedrooms. All the bedrooms are relatively small, a strategy that gets family members out of their rooms and into the shared living space. The master bedroom is on the main floor and has a private deck that looks out over the woods. RoseMary and Herb like the sense of privacy they have in their room. The children's bedrooms are located directly above the master bedroom, just up a short flight of stairs. Although the children's bedrooms are decidedly compact, built-in desks, bookshelves, and trundle beds make the rooms attractive, efficient, and pleasant.

Their new home continues to please and delight the Pilhofers, and they love the easy-going way of life they have found here. It's a home that honors family heritage while supporting a modern American lifestyle.

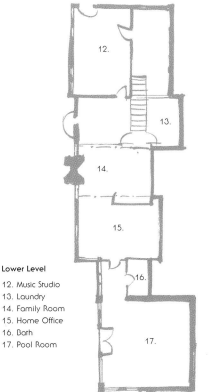

Main Floor

1. Entry
2. Great Room
3. Kitchen
4. Dining
5. Master Bedroom
6. Bath
7. Screen Porch
8. Deck
9. Garage

Lower Level

12. Music Studio
13. Laundry
14. Family Room
15. Home Office
16. Bath
17. Pool Room

is there life without a lawn?

Their new home is everything that RoseMary Januschka and Herb Pilhofer had hoped that it would be: compact, informal, and easy to maintain. One thing is decidedly missing—there is no lawn here, not a single blade of cultivated grass.

"At our old place, it was six hours a week, just to keep the lawn up," remembers Herb. According to the Pilhofers, if you move into a pine forest, it makes sense to let the forest come right up to the door. After the home was finished, the Pilhofers restored the ground that had been disturbed during construction and threw out a variety of wildflower seeds. "We have wild turkeys, deer, and a couple of coyotes out here," says RoseMary. "It's great for our kids to grow up in an untouched pine forest."

wenty-five years ago, when Chris and Gene Callahan were newlyweds and just starting out, they purchased their first home. It was an 850-sq.-ft. condemned two-bedroom "cottage" with only one thing to recommend it—they could afford to buy it. "We set to work remodeling it," remembers Chris, "and saw it transformed into a pretty charming place. We had our two children while we lived there."

Fast forward to the present. The Callahans are now respected builders who specialize in creating finely crafted homes for their

Starting Small,
Dreaming Big

clients. When Gene and Chris recently acquired an old apple orchard, they decided to hold onto the property and build a few rental units. The first project was to be a little bungalow, something just right for a young couple starting out—a couple like they had been 25 years ago. The house was to be small and affordable, pared down but full of well-chosen materials and fine craftsmanship. It was to be a place where a new family could grow and flourish.

It's All in the Details

Designing and building a small family home on a tight budget requires a clear focus on the essentials. The basic design of this bungalow—the simple floorplan, shed-style dormer, and overall low height—works effectively to contain construction costs, one of the Callahans' primary considerations.

The house is tiny by today's standards, but rather than using up all their resources on square footage, Gene and Chris chose to invest in

Above **In the damp northern California climate, broad overhangs provide welcome protection from the elements. The shed roofline extends beyond the footprint of the house to create a cost-conscious carport.**

Right **Nestled in an old orchard, this charming shingled, Craftsman-style bungalow might draw its inspiration from Snow White's cottage. Sturdily constructed, it is a compact starter home that features the high level of craftsmanship and attention to detail usually found in much larger, grander homes.**

Opposite *Although the great room is small by most standards, the 18-ft. vaulted ceiling and massive Palladian-style window wall give a surprising sense of spaciousness. The inlaid blackboard slate entryway is framed in naturally glazed tiles and trimmed with black walnut.*

Top right *The oversize trim elements give this house a sense of solidity and security. Using large trim pieces on a house this small makes it appear to be almost larger than life.*

exceptionally fine materials and a high level of craftsmanship. It was a decision born out of the Callahans' belief that less can definitely be more—it's all in the details. Despite its seeming modesty, the Callahans' cottage is as thoughtfully conceived as larger, grander homes. "It turns out that doing things the right way doesn't mean it's going to take a lot more time or cost a lot more money," asserts Gene. "For example, we staggered the shingles, which adds a lot to the visual appeal. It was maybe one extra second per shingle to position it either up or down. To me, it's worth it."

From the vertical board skirting that covers the home's foundation to the custom-milled 3-in.-thick rafters, trim details have been thoughtfully considered to give the house a charming storybook look. The Callahans carefully considered where to economize and when to splurge. The vinyl windows they chose to contain costs, for example, are divided lights trimmed out with 6 in.

of solid wood. Hardwood floors are black oak trimmed in black walnut, both indigenous, locally harvested woods. The kitchen cabinets, custom built for Gene by cabinetmaker Harry Carlson, are solid walnut. The walnut is from a tree that Gene cut and milled with his portable sawmill.

A Big Space on a Small Footprint

Despite its small scale, the cottage's open design provides a small family with generously sized living quarters and a comfortable place to gather—perhaps the single most important feature in any family home. A grand, Palladian-style wall of windows floods the cottage's great room with sunshine. The compact kitchen opens onto the great room to continue the easy flow of the space, and it, too, features a vaulted ceiling.

Just as families need a central gathering place, individual family members need to be able to withdraw from family activities. A hand-wrought, solid-walnut balustrade lines the stairs that lead to the second-floor master bedroom. From the beginning, the Callahans knew they wanted to build a two-bedroom cottage; the idea to place the master bedroom on the second floor was a solution that allows for a little privacy. "I especially would have loved that upstairs bedroom in our early years—a small retreat from the daily activities of the main floor," says Chris.

Home, Sweet Home

Since the day it was finished, the Callahans' cottage has been rented by a young couple who fell in love with the place at first sight. With Gene and Chris's permission, they took on a building project of their own: a glass-enclosed artist's studio. Recently, the tenants became first-time parents—just the family that Gene and Chris had in mind from the day they started planning the pretty little house.

Above **The richness of detailing extends into every room of the house. In the kitchen, solid walnut custom cabinetry, clear fir window trim, black oak flooring, and ceramic tile countertops imbue the space with a rich warmth.**

Opposite **Funky but functional. The tenants erected this artist's studio as a lean-to built out from an existing shed. A potpourri of found materials contributes to the whimsical, impromptu feeling of the space.**

serendipity by design

"The whole house was a work in progress," observes Gene. "I drew up a plan that could get a building permit, and I went from there. I didn't know exactly what it was going to look like until I was done—that was part of the fun for me."

Case in point, a carpenter friend came by the building site one day with the news that a local school was throwing away all of its old blackboards. Thinking that it might be nice to use a little slate, Gene stopped what he was doing and drove on over to the school where he found the old slate boards in a stack by the dumpsters. "On one side, they were smooth, of course, but the backs were unfinished, just roughly split, with fish fossils still in them. Really lovely." The slate was salvaged on the spot, and part of Gene's haul was transformed into the wood stove's hearth.

Main Floor

1. Entry
2. Living Room
3. Kitchen
4. Dining Nook
5. Bedroom
6. Bath
7. Deck
8. Carport

At first glance, Grace Gordon-Collins, Ernest Collins, and their two children could be any typical nuclear family—mom, dad, and a couple of teenage kids. But take a closer look, because their home in rural British Columbia was designed to support a very nontraditional lifestyle. When they first bought their property in this mountain valley several years ago, the Collins thought that all they were after was a nice little weekend place. Before long, however, Grace and Ernie realized that what they really wanted was a life outside the city for themselves and their children.

Home for the Weekend

Partners in business as well as in marriage for almost 30 years, the Collins run architectural and design firm offices three hours to the south in Vancouver. Each spends alternating weeks in the city overseeing business interests, while the other partner works out of their well-equipped home office and keeps the home fires burning. "Ernie and I are together here every weekend," says Grace. "Our son is away at college, and our daughter attends the local high school. At this point, she's the only full-time resident." Within the next few years, the home will increasingly become the Collins' full-time base for business, but in the meantime, it must accommodate their busy here-again-gone-again routine.

"Design is a process of negotiation," reflects Ernie. "You must constantly balance each other's wishes and desires, tempering all of it with the financial constraints." While they disagreed about some of the details, from the very start Grace and Ernie were in complete agreement about the basics. The home they envisioned was to be a place where the walls between themselves and their children should (quite literally) be down, where their personal and professional lives could be better integrated, and where they could relax.

Above **Northern light from the vaulted entry dramatizes the cathedral-like ceiling and spills over into the great room. The massive roof trusses are made from old-growth fir timbers salvaged from a Vancouver warehouse.**

Opposite **Furniture groups, light fixtures, and custom cabinets delineate the space, creating "rooms" within the larger room where family and friends can gather in comfort.**

Left *The second-floor catwalk emphasizes the grand proportions and airy volume of the great room while streamlining the commute to work. The penetration of the office tower into the great room and its open passageway are design strategies that integrate work life into home life.*

Above **This "Morning Star" window of cut and leaded glass was created for the owners by a local artist.**

Opposite, top right **Kitchen cabinets, open shelves, and a work island provide a sleek center for food preparation and double as a place to display the owners' collections of baskets, glassware, and family mementos.**

Opposite, bottom right **The kitchen faces out from the corner of the great room, with a panoramic view of the home's central gathering area.**

We're All in This Together

"We've always loved big open spaces, barns, and cathedrals, and that's what we wanted," Ernie says of the enormous great room at the center of the house. A full three stories from the hardwood floors to the peak of the roof, it's a light-filled expanse with views of mountains that ring the valley. Design features, lighting fixtures, and furniture all work to define the space, so that even without the familiar context of separate rooms, the space easily fulfills its varied functions.

In a home where either Mom or Dad must be away for significant periods of time, it's essential that the space itself works overtime to promote family ties. For the Collins, that means that even when everyone is pursuing separate activities, they are still together as a family, connected by the room itself. "We all tend to live in the great room," says Grace. "Our daughter might be watching a video while Ernie and I are sitting in front of the fire with our feet up or one of us is cooking dinner. The sheer volume of the space keeps one activity from encroaching onto the next, but when we look up, we're all together."

Catwalk to Work

Stairs in the great room lead to the children's second-floor bedrooms, with an art-lined catwalk continuing on to Grace and Ernie's offices. While some homeowners don't require much more from a home office than a place to do a little paperwork, the Collins needed to dedicate a significant portion of their resources to constructing professional-quality office space in their new home. They knew that the public rooms of the house could also work for client meetings and business entertaining, but to make the transition that they envisioned, they needed adequate studio space for two busy, successful architects.

Rather than build a completely separate structure, Grace and Ernie put their offices in a three-story tower that abuts one corner of the great room. Originally, the Collins planned to set up separate offices, but they

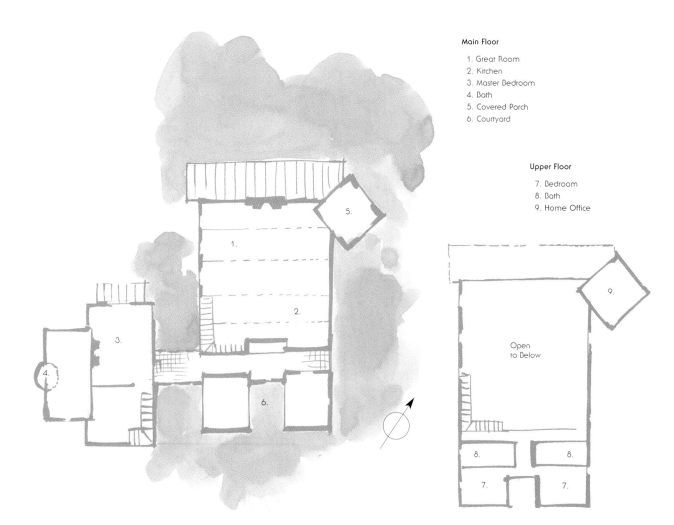

Main Floor

1. Great Room
2. Kitchen
3. Master Bedroom
4. Bath
5. Covered Porch
6. Courtyard

Upper Floor

7. Bedroom
8. Bath
9. Home Office

Open to Below

have since found it to be a more efficient use of resources to share the tower's second-floor office while using third-floor space as a library and meeting room. Ernie and Grace agree that placing their work space in an adjacent tower keeps them close—but not too close—to family activities. "The catwalk gives a bit of a promenade to get to the office," notes Ernie. "But there's no door to close it off. It's enough of a separation, but still part of what's going on in the rest of the house."

The Family Sanctuary

The Collins treasure the way their home easily accommodates work and relaxation and the comings and goings of family, friends, neighbors, and clients. "But when you have this kind of open living

Right **A tower annex in the form of a grain elevator (left) and a round silo with a conical roof (far right) evoke the farm architecture that surrounds this house in its rural setting. The home was designed around a three-story central great room that is warmed by a massive hearth. (Photo by Roger Brooks)**

Left *The master bedroom's walls were ragged with two shades of mellow gold to harmonize with the carpeting and bedding. The overall feeling is of softness and warmth.*

Opposite *Elegant appointments, comfortable furniture, and an antique clawfoot tub create a private sanctuary in the heart of the family home.*

Below *An imposing hand-carved antique cabinet serves as a linen closet in the master bathroom. The fringed massage table was custom-crafted by the owner.*

arrangement, you need one perfectly private space," notes Grace. The master suite is down its own art-lined hallway. Past the serene master bedroom with its fireplace at the foot of the bed and a spacious dressing room lined with closets is the inviting master bathroom. This is a space that the whole family uses for bathing, relaxing, and massage.

"My daughter might come visit while I'm in the tub, or I'll drink my morning coffee and talk to Ernie while he's in the shower," observes Grace. Completely out of the traffic patterns of the house, it is the space most removed from the public realm—the end of the road on the jour-

making their mark

"We named our place Morning Star," says Grace Gordon-Collins of the country home she shares with her husband Ernest and their two children. The choice is both a tribute to the beauty of the sky in their mountain valley and an acknowledgment of their decision to move away from an urban lifestyle. The theme is carried throughout the house, with stars as an element in leaded windows, fabrics, and furniture.

The house itself was the Collins' first link to the community. Ernie was a hands-on contractor who hired local craftsmen for much of the construction. The housewarming party was a community affair. With branding irons forged by a local blacksmith, the entire neighborhood turned out to help Grace and Ernie brand their Morning Star into outside furniture and decks.

ney that Ernie and Grace are making from Vancouver. While many people choose to include second private family rooms in their new homes—most often libraries, project spaces, or dedicated media rooms—the Collins created this master bathroom as their private sanctuary. With its intimate seating area and all the appointments of a luxury spa, this is the place where they can fully relax and focus on themselves and each other.

While the Collins have yet to completely shift their business base from the city to their new home in the country, their house is up to the challenge. In the meantime, they appreciate how well it is functioning throughout the long transition. "As an architect, you think in terms of frameworks," reflects Grace, "and in that, I think our home works beautifully. The details will always have a way of working out, because the framework is so right."

Above **A riding saddle doubles as a work of art when displayed in the great room.**

Opposite **The intimately lit table is a cozy counterpoint to the great outdoors.**

The owners of this beach house decided to leave Los Angeles and find a tranquil, natural setting in which to raise their two small daughters. They made the move in increments, first renting a house near the beach outside Santa Barbara. They quickly discovered how much they loved the area and the easy-going beach lifestyle. The couple purchased an existing house and called on architect Andy Neumann, well known for his beach houses, to help them remodel it. At the eleventh hour, however, they realized that the house would never be what they really wanted for their family, so they canceled the remod-

By the Beautiful Sea

eling project. Eventually, they purchased an ocean-front lot, and once again they called on Andy, this time to design their ideal family home from the ground up.

The owners wanted their new home to be user-friendly, private, and beach oriented. It was to be a functional place where the kids could have fun, where they would all be comfortable, and where family and friends would always be welcome. They wanted a cottage-scaled house with a variety of living spaces—open, expansive rooms that would take in the sweeping view of the California coastline, as well as intimate nooks where parents and children could cuddle up together to read storybooks.

It was important to the owners that every room in the house be used and enjoyed and that family heirlooms be integrated into the everyday life of the home. They required a separate, private office for the husband, as well as a home office for the wife that wouldn't isolate her from the children. And finally, they wanted a place of honor for their vintage piano and a high, peaked ceiling so that they could put up a really big Christmas tree every December.

Above **Through the front entry, French doors on the opposite wall lead directly out to the beach. The owners wanted the ocean's presence to be immediately seen and experienced.**

Opposite **The living room's vaulted ceiling increases the sense of spaciousness and light. Area rugs define two distinct seating areas and create a pathway that leads to the bedroom wing. A recess creates a place of honor for a vintage piano, a wedding gift from the bride to the groom.**

Left **An eating bar with drop lights defines the boundary between the kitchen and the informal family room. The cabinet's built-in bookcase holds a collection of cookbooks.**

Opposite, top **A walk-through closet is shared by the sisters. Built-in storage units, mirrored on either side, keep clothes well organized.**

Opposite, bottom **The children's bathroom takes its cue from beach cabanas. Bright seaside colors, open towel storage, and a row of pegs create a clean, cheerful space.**

Opposite *The color palette of the house finds its inspiration in the ocean and the beach. Here, a custom-made china cupboard connects the kitchen to the formal dining room beyond.*

All in the Family

The home that Andy designed for this family is a quintessential beach house, reminiscent of the shingled Cape-style beach cottages found on Martha's Vineyard but with a decidedly sophisticated California feel. To the couple that lives here, life is all about family, having fun together, and creating happy memories, so no place in this home is off-limits to the children and their friends. Public rooms are informal, and materials are durable and easy to maintain.

The home is built along two intersecting hallways (places where children everywhere enjoy playing—and very much the case here), and each room features views of the ocean and the surrounding wetlands. French doors in the living room, dining room, family room, and master suite all open onto an expansive deck, where steps lead directly to the beach.

The living room and formal dining room flank the entry hallway, making up the center of the home. All four sets of the children's great-grandparents are represented here, either in photographs on the walls or in the furniture that the family uses and enjoys every day. Beyond the dining room, the integrated family room/kitchen features a spacious central work island. While the kitchen can comfortably accommodate multiple cooks, the homeowners requested the work island for social reasons—it became a favorite spot for family and friends to gather around for snacking, chatting, and visiting with the cook.

The master suite shares a bedroom wing with the children's bedrooms, although parents are separated from kids by a library hallway and a short flight of stairs. It's enough distance for Mom and Dad to have a sense of their own privacy, but not so much that the girls feel isolated. The girls' bedrooms are placed side by side and are connected by a large, shared closet.

Although the girls' rooms were originally planned as two separate bedrooms, the girls enjoy a close relationship and chose to use one room for sleeping and the other room for play. As they grow older, it's likely they'll want the privacy of separate bedrooms once again. Above the bedrooms, a loft play space is tucked up under the eaves. The loft features a railing and louvered doors at one end that open out over the stairway and landing. A "secret" play area like this utilizes otherwise unused space in a house, but more important, it is a special hideaway that a child will use, cherish, and remember forever.

A Tale of Two Offices

This house features two variations on home offices, and each one fulfills a very different purpose. The wife needed a place to take care of household paperwork, bill paying, and correspondence, and she asked that the office not isolate her from the children. Rather than giving her an alcove in the family room or a small desk in the kitchen—solutions often seen in family homes—Andy placed her office and an adjoining sitting area for the children on the stairway and landings that lead to the girls' bedrooms.

When Mom is working at her desk, the girls are often nearby in their sitting area, playing or doing their homework. Everyone likes having Mom right there in case she's needed, but because she is right there, the kids typically leave her alone so she can get her work done.

The husband, a writer, needed office space that placed him well away from the distractions of family activities. While he originally asked

Above *Location is everything. The generous deck extends the living spaces to take full advantage of the spectacular setting and features built-in seating and a glass windbreak. Beyond the boardwalk, the standalone office commands a sweeping view of the ocean.*

Opposite *There's no wasted space in this hallway between bedrooms. The library was placed here to integrate the owners' collections of books and family photos into the daily flow of family life.*

Years ago, the owners of this house built themselves a little summer cottage on Martha's Vineyard, where both had spent happy days as children. Its single source of heat was a wood stove; the shower was just outside the back door. When the wife became pregnant with their first child, the husband began working on a design to enlarge, improve, and winterize the cottage. Architect Peter Breese was a friend of a friend. The couple approached him simply to ask if he would draft their design ideas into a set of blueprints.

Family Dream Home

At first, Peter made suggestions for a few improvements to their design, and the couple liked what he had to say. They explained to Peter that they planned on having three children and what they really wanted was a house that could grow with their family. Most important, the center of the home needed to be a large, expansive living area, a place where everyone could be together.

Inspired by their vision, Peter had more ideas to share with the owners. Ultimately, the original plans for the cottage expansion were scrapped and the cottage was moved elsewhere on the property to make way for an all-new family home. Today, the young couple are the parents of three growing, active children, just as they had hoped they would be. And the house that Peter designed for them is their beloved family home.

Above **The large roof overhangs and long horizontal lines help make this house feel close to the ground. The home's shiplike cluster of forms was inspired by the ferry that brings the family to their home on Martha's Vineyard.**

Right **Kids swing away the summer on the porch and tree swings. The guest cottage (the original cabin built by the homeowners) is just visible through the trees.**

Opposite *A huge window seat easily accommodates the entire family for evening storytime. Large casement windows open wide to bring in the sea breeze.*

Right *A true great room, the kitchen, dining, and living areas are all part of one expansive space. A runner carpet delineates the living room from the dining room and leads to French doors and the deck beyond. The lower ceiling in the kitchen breaks up the volume and brings the space into scale.*

Open Space for an Active Family

The living room, dining area, and kitchen share a single great room where a wall of windows takes in the view of woods, water, and sky. The post-and-beam construction has been left partially exposed, which gives definition to the large space and adds a casual, informal look.

This is the center of activity for this active family, and, according to the homeowners, their children thrive in an environment where Mom and Dad are usually in plain view. In their turn, the parents like being able to see their children playing in the living room when they look up from working in the kitchen. An enormous window seat in the living area is a favorite spot for family reading time, board games, and occasional impromptu theatrical performances (with blankets hung between the posts for curtains).

Outside and In

Windows and doors in the great room open to a broad wraparound deck, a favorite play area for the children. The deck is low to the ground, just a step up from the broad green lawn beyond. On one end of the deck, an enclosed screen porch is used for summertime meals. A pass-through directly from the kitchen to the screen porch streamlines serving and cleanup.

The wraparound deck is used by everyone in the family, and, as in the great room, there's room on the deck for more than one activity at a time. A broad overhang provides shade when the sun is hot as well as protection from summer rainstorms. Comfortable, oversized rocking chairs, an old-fashioned porch swing, and a curved railing that doubles as a bench provide ample seating.

A cozy family room on the first floor is a space away from all the activity. The television was relegated to the family room so that it wouldn't intrude on family time in the great room. Doors from the family room open directly into the kitchen and a first-floor bathroom. "The children can come and go to the kitchen and the bathroom from the family room without having to make a major appearance in the living spaces," says Peter. According to the homeowners, their children are still young enough to want to be near their parents, but in a few more years, the family room may well become the perfect teen hideaway.

Sleepover Heaven

Upstairs, the two girls share a large bedroom. Captain's beds feature built-in storage drawers and open shelves. Railings on the beds are a safety feature that can be removed when the children are older. Above each bed, a loft provides a special hideaway and an extra bunk when friends come for sleepovers. The son has his

Above **Food and dishes take a short cut at mealtime. The pass-through from the kitchen to the screen porch saves on steps. Incorporating conveniences like this into the design of the home is an effective strategy for encouraging the full use of the house.**

Opposite **The curve of the deck is echoed in the curve of the bench. The wave-like shape reinforces the nautical flavor of the overall design. The turned columns were salvaged from an old Victorian home.**

Left *The bright, airy master bedroom is a sanctuary away from the children. A private deck for sunny mornings and a fireplace for chilly evenings make this a place apart from the rest of the home. The painting is by a grandparent.*

Right, top *A pair of captain's beds and sleeping lofts provide a comfortable space for slumber parties and visiting cousins. Ample built-in shelves and storage drawers help manage clutter.*

Right, bottom *The colorful finishes in the children's bathroom are durable and fun. The stacked washer and dryer share the space. When the children are old enough, it will be easy for them to assume their own wash-day responsibilities.*

own small bedroom, which was originally used as the nursery when the children were babies.

The children share a large bathroom that doubles as the family's laundry room. A stacked washer and dryer conserves space and shares a wall with counter space and cupboards. The choice of placing the washer and dryer on the second floor may

mean extra trips up and down the stairs during the day, but most of the family's laundry—clothing and bath towels—remains near bedrooms and bathroom.

Main Floor

1. Stair Hall
2. Living Room
3. Dining Room
4. Kitchen
5. Screen Porch
6. Family Room
7. Bath
8. Studio
9. Storage

Living the Dream

The idealized home that the couple dreamed of when the wife was pregnant with their first child has taken on a life of its own. The staircase they envisioned as a beautiful, artistic focal point has become one of their children's favorite places to play. Their gracious great room is sometimes an indoor gymnasium, littered with plastic vehicles and doll strollers. And quiet moments together sharing the view of a romantic sunset are usually interrupted by handstand contests in the breezeway. Family life is everything they ever dreamed it would be.

Above **Choice of wall color, easygoing furniture, and relaxed decor are beach cottage style. The fireplace surround was designed by the homeowners.**

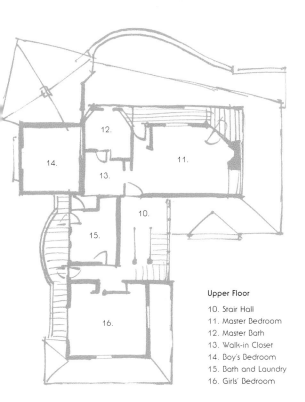

keeping the dirt out

In this active family, everyone spends a great deal of time outdoors. Favorite summertime activities include swimming and surf fishing. In his design, architect Peter Breese included a strategy for getting wet and tired children back into the house while leaving most of the sand and dirt outside. Inspiration came from the homeowners' original outdoor shower, which has been incorporated into a bulkhead in the backyard. An exterior stairway leads directly from the backyard to the second-floor family bathroom/laundry room.

"The scenario is that wet and sandy children and their parents shower outside, come up the stairs, leave the wet swimsuits on the balcony rail in the sun, run through the bath, grab a dry towel at the laundry, and go on into the various bedrooms," explains Peter.

Upper Floor

10. Stair Hall
11. Master Bedroom
12. Master Bath
13. Walk-in Closet
14. Boy's Bedroom
15. Bath and Laundry
16. Girls' Bedroom

Twenty years ago, a Charleston couple purchased a 1,000-acre parcel in the low country of South Carolina to use as a weekend retreat for themselves and their seven children. The location had a special significance, because their family had historic ties to the area—in fact, over a hundred years ago, one particular grandfather farmed the land directly across the river. The land consisted of wetlands, hardwood forests, and broken fields, and the owners eventually established it as a wildlife preserve. They put the land into a perpetual easement so that it could never be divided. This is a legacy they have created to pass on to their children and their children's children.

A Home for the Generations

As one by one their children left the nest and began families of their own, the couple began to consider the lifestyle they wanted during their retirement years. Ultimately, they decided that what they wanted was a place where the whole clan could gather, a place that was refined but decidedly casual. Rather than staying on in Charleston, they realized that they could create everything they wanted at their country property.

The home was to sit on a commanding bluff, with views out over the river and the land. It was to have large, open living spaces that could graciously accommodate gatherings of their large family, as well as a smaller space that would be a comfortable nest when it was just the two of them. Most important, the house was to express a sense of their history as a family and their abiding ties to the land.

Above **The cluster of buildings set along the edge of a field under trees that line a riverbank evokes a classic Southern plantation.**

Right **Salvaged timbers give the great room a sense of dignity and history. A large pass-through and a pair of pocket doors open to the kitchen/den beyond.**

Opposite **The pavilion features an exposed "king-post" truss system and the same round brick columns used on the porches. An outdoor living "room" for large family gatherings, the pavilion provides welcome shade and captures the breezes off the river.**

Right **The brick end walls of the main house are evocative of early Dutch settlements in South Carolina. Decorative coursework breaks up the wall and ties into the eaves. Columns at either side add definition. Some of the bricks used at the foundation level and on the patios were salvaged from local ruins.**

Traditional Values and Flexible Spaces

In architect Virginia Duncan Lane, the couple found a sympathetic collaborator who was enthusiastic about designing an up-to-date home that honored the past. She designed a home in which the forms are reminiscent of early plantations but detailed with a contemporary sensibility.

Handmade brick end walls echo the homes of early Dutch settlers and feature decorative brick courses. Broad, antebellum-style porches provide shade and catch the breeze off the river on even the most sultry summer afternoons. An open pavilion reconsiders the home's round brick columns and proportions and presents them as a large outdoor "room" suited for family-style entertaining and relaxing. Built as a gathering of structures, the house looks almost like an old-time farmstead, built for a family and added onto over the generations.

The center of the house is an enormous living hall, rich with native cypress paneling, the wood salvaged from an old dock near Savannah. Because the homeowners put an especially high value on creating opportunities for the whole family to gather together, the great room features a large central seating area around the hearth (rather than several smaller groupings of furniture) and an expansive dining table that can comfortably accommodate a crowd. The room itself is intentionally free of any alcoves or window seats that might tend to isolate people into small groups.

Clerestory and dormer windows flood the room with daylight. Divided-light windows and doors line three sides of the great room and offer ever-changing views of fields, woodlands, and the river. The kitchen/den, technically a separate room, opens to the great room through a pair of pocket doors and a large central pass-through, to become a seamless extension of the great room.

A Place of Their Own

When children and grandchildren have come and gone, the homeowners typically close off the great room and move family life into the kitchen/den. They enjoy the coziness of the space when it is just the two of them and have found that the room is just the right size for intimate, small-scale entertaining as well. This design allows the cook in the kitchen to be an integral part of the conversation and the company. Rich woods, granite countertops, and weathered bricks create a warm and inviting environment.

Hallways lead from the kitchen/den to the master suite and guest wing. The master suite opens onto a private walled garden, a space that is truly the couple's inner sanctum. The homeowners' children and grandchildren all have standing invitations, so the guest wing is frequently occupied. The guest wing was carefully situated so that it doesn't share any walls with the master suite. Even when the house is full of family, the master suite affords the homeowners a

Below **In contrast to the rich wood of the wall paneling and exposed wooden trusses, the white ceiling reflects light from the dormer windows and the band of narrow clerestory windows.**

Above **The kitchen/den opens to the great room through a broad pass-through and passageways on either side, all of which can be closed with louvered pocket doors. The custom cabinets, made of longleaf Southern pine, perfectly fill the space and are an important element of the architecture of the room.**

Right **The large great room is made cozy by rich wood paneling and flooring and by carefully selected period furnishings. Built-in bookcases and a dramatic wrought-iron chandelier add warmth and charm.**

ohn and Kathy Cook's home was a perfect fit. Designed by O'Neil Pennoyer Architects, they had purchased it from the builder shortly after its completion. Although it wasn't custom built, Kathy and John always appreciated how well it suited both their tastes and their needs. When their daughter was born, however, the features that made their house perfect for a professional couple with no children were suddenly keeping it from being a good fit for their new child-centered family lifestyle.

Where before they enjoyed entertaining in their very formal living and dining rooms, the Cooks now wanted spaces where they could be comfortable with their daughter every day. Rather than

At Home on the Hill

having a master suite that was their private sanctuary away from the outside world, they now needed a master bedroom that preserved their sense of retreat while putting them close to their child's bedroom. They wanted comfortable guest quarters for visiting family, separate office spaces for each of them, and a playroom for their growing daughter.

Rather than remodel their existing house, Kathy and John decided to create a home that would be right for their family from the ground up. They found a private, wooded lot on top of a small hill. Located in a suburb outside Boston, it was the perfect setting in which to raise their daughter. Choosing an architect can be stressful, but the Cooks had no need to conduct interviews or collect references. They eagerly brought their ideas directly to architects David O'Neil and Sheldon Pennoyer.

The Center of Things

The center of their new family home is a great room that features heavy post-and-beam construction. The extensive use of natural woods, a

Above **Hipped roofs and a banding course atop the first-floor windows help to control the scale of the house. Broad overhangs keep rain off the screen-porch windows.**

Right **The screen porch functions as an important sitting and dining area in warm weather. The plant shelf is a great place for vegetable starts in the spring, as well as a favorite hangout for the family cats.**

Above *This small music room is a private retreat for the homeowners. Windows are set low to the floor to let in the view of the woods.*

Opposite *Sturdy timbers, a cathedral ceiling, and a wall of stone play up the scale of the great room, while warm rugs and informal furnishings add coziness and comfort to the space. The second-floor balcony on the right leads to the guest suite and provides a wonderful view into the heart of the house.*

massive fieldstone fireplace with a raised hearth, and generous windows with deep sills (specially requested as a favor for their cats) combine to give the great room a warm, country look. The great room is the focal point, the central living area surrounded by the rest of the house. According to architect David O'Neil, this type of central living space has a way of attracting people to it, and it is a hallmark of a well-conceived family home.

Despite the room's grand proportions, there is real coziness here. Comfortable, oversized furniture is grouped for conversation in front of the fireplace, which is where the Cook family spends a great deal of their time. There is no television in the great room. Instead, a game table is set up to one side, the perfect spot for board games, a favorite family activity. Much of the Cooks' entertaining is small scale, and the great room is just right for cocktails, after-dinner conversation, or a friendly game of bridge.

Living within the Balance

The careful balance between communal and private spaces is always an important consideration for a family home, as are the demands that family members place on those spaces. Kathy's full-time office, for example, is a snug library with wrap-around bookcases. Located just beyond the great room, it gives her the separation she requires to concentrate on work without undue isolation from home and family. The library features the same post-and-beam construction and fieldstone hearth as the great room, which visually connects the space to the rest of the house.

John's home office, on the other hand, is used primarily for personal projects and weekend catchup. It's on the basement level adjacent to the playroom. Accordingly, the Cooks' daughter might choose to draw in the library while Kathy is working during the day and head down to her playroom in the evenings or on weekends when John is nearby in his office.

Girl's World

From their very first conversation with the architects, the Cooks asked that their new home be a special environment for their daughter, and the house is full of features designed to delight any child. The girl's bedroom features a small "inner sanctum," a little space under the eaves that might otherwise have been walled off. A 4-ft.-high door provides kid-size access. According to Kathy and John, their daughter loves having this "secret" hideaway and plays in it frequently. In future years, this little room will be useful as storage space.

The basement-level playroom has a full wall of windows and is the kind of open, indoor play space where a kid can be a kid. There's room here for playing with big toys, watching videos, and hanging out with friends. The screen porch off the kitchen is a favorite spot during the warm summer months for quiet-time activities.

"The architects came up with something really unique for our daughter, and we just love it," says Kathy. It is a special, two-story playhouse complete with working windows and a bird's-eye view. The playhouse is an architectural feature of the house as well. It visually separates the front of the house from access to the garage and stands like a small watchtower over the front courtyard.

The Cooks' home works for their family. Says John, "I think this house will see us through to retirement. There's room here to spread out and be comfortable. And the great room is a place that keeps pulling everyone together. The first week we moved into the house, it felt as if we'd already been here for ten years—it's that comfortable."

Above, top **Built-in linen storage lines the second-floor hallway.**

Above, bottom **The fortlike playhouse at the edge of the courtyard was built for the owners' daughter.**

Opposite **The library's stone hearth is framed by post-and-beam timbers and flanked by floor-to-ceiling bookshelves. This well-appointed space is used as a full-time home office.**

A couple with four young children came to architect Fu Tung Cheng with the dream of building a tranquil home in the country. The home they envisioned was an informal place where family activities would be centered around a well-integrated living space. The couple wanted to take advantage of the mild California climate by using the outdoors as well as the indoors. The home would be fun and comfortable for the children, but with tough materials and durable finishes that would stand up to the wear and tear of daily family life. Above all, the home would be uniquely beautiful, a place the family could call their own.

Timeless Beauty
for a Modern Family

When Fu Tung learned that the couple planned to build for the long term, he set about designing a home that could respond to more than just the family's immediate needs. He focused on creating flexible spaces and building in strategies that would enable the house to expand over time. He took into account not only who the four children were as youngsters, but what they might need as teenagers.

A New Tradition

The home fuses post-and-beam architecture with an Asian sense of beauty through simplicity; it is reminiscent of Japanese farmhouses in the eaves and the roofline. The three-story water tower wing and the corrugated metal exterior siding, familiar elements of the American barn, fit the house comfortably into its rural setting. At the center of the home, the living room, dining room,

Above *Unusual angles and geometric forms combine with commonplace building materials to create a unique vision of a rural family home. The three-story tower houses the family bathrooms.*

Right *Post-and-beam trusses, an inset hardwood floor, and the placement of simple, elegant furnishings all come together in a space that is well defined but fluid. The Asian-style lattice roof framing is reflected in the shape of the windows.*

Above **The mudroom features storage and low-mounted coat hooks for kids. The vintage office door leads directly into the center of the house. Crown molding and fluted casings give a nod to the past.**

Left, top **The absence of wall cabinets in the kitchen makes room for a band of eye-level windows above the sink. A huge central skylight directly above the dining table and the kitchen work island floods the space with natural light.**

Left, bottom **A long inlaid pathway of maple flooring softens the transition between the living and kitchen areas.**

family room, and kitchen form a refined variation on the great room concept. The fir-clad steel columns of the post-and-beam framework give added definition to the space. The family typically gathers around the dining room table or in the living room, where they read, visit, and play.

Throughout, eclectic materials are used in unexpected ways. An inlaid vertical-grain fir floor divides the space visually, while floors in the kitchen, dining, and living areas are of poured concrete with marble-piece inlays. The kitchen includes an oversized work island with poured concrete countertops that feature Fu Tung's signature inlay work. The enormous work island provides plenty of room for meal preparation and is a favorite perch for snacking, homework, and arts and crafts activities. Dishes are stored beneath the island on open shelves. With everything easily accessible and free from the potential hazard of swinging cupboard doors, even the youngest child can participate in table setting and kitchen cleanup.

Designed for Change

The family room is tucked in a corner—a private place for quiet-time activities. Above the family room, mudroom, and pantry, there's an open space that could be transformed into a teen loft someday. "There's a tremendous amount of space here—Fu Tung really pushed us on that, and I'm glad he did," says the husband.

Just off the formal entrance, a flight of stairs leads to the master suite, which features a sitting area that takes in the view. "There's still some up and down the stairs at night to tend to the kids," says the wife, "but that's fading, and it's been worth the trade-off for the sense of privacy and retreat we have up here." A small second-floor room is currently used as a combination guest room and study. Eventually, this may become a bedroom for the oldest child, who is beginning to lobby his parents for more privacy. A third-floor space above the master bath remains unfinished but might someday become a home office or a gym. If the owners ever decide that the family needs even more space, there's also room to build out over the garage.

Shared Spaces

Down on the main floor, the four children share two generously sized bedrooms, one for the boys and one for the girls. The trend toward shared spaces works particularly well here because of a connecting closet that provides a place to park big toys, toy bins, and sports equipment. It is also an additional passageway that leads directly between the two bedrooms. The kids love the traffic flow that this layout establishes.

Even though the children are still relatively young, the distance between parents' and children's bedrooms hasn't been a significant problem; feelings of isolation are infrequent for siblings who are

Above **The master bedroom is simple and serene. A built-in dresser and a walk-in closet maximize space and minimize clutter by eliminating horizontal surfaces. The sitting area looks out over the view.**

Right **The children's bathroom is streamlined and easy to keep clean. Cement floor and countertops are a durable, unusual choice for a family bathroom. A tile baseboard softens the transition between wall and floor.**

hen Tom and Dorothy Stormont approached architect Michaela Mahady, their heartfelt request was for a home that would function well for their young family. The house where they'd been living was 1960s modern and had definitely been designed without a family in mind—no mudroom, no playroom, and a kitchen that was on the second floor. The Stormonts knew from first-hand experience how difficult it was to live in a place that did not provide adequate spaces for the needs and activities of their family. What they wanted for themselves and their children was a home carefully designed to make family life easy, convenient, comfortable, and fun.

Life on the River

The Stormonts wanted a kitchen that was at the very heart of their home, a kitchen that the whole family could share. They asked for a comfortable eating/family space where everyone could gather. Tom and Dorothy knew they needed an old-fashioned mudroom where their three active children could simply kick off their tennis shoes before they ever tracked dirt and mud into the house. And they especially wanted a great playroom, a generous, out-of-the-way space with decent sound insulation where the kids could hoot and holler, play catch with their stuffed animals, and turn somersaults on the wall-to-wall carpeting.

Control Central

Just as they requested, the very center of the Stormonts' new home is their kitchen. "This is control central," says Tom. It was carefully sited to be convenient to every other room in the house. To one side, stairs lead down to a sunken living room and formal dining room that the family use primarily for television viewing

Above **The massive gables of the main house and the adjoining garage make this home feel stable and solid— a safe place to raise a family.**

Right **Broad French doors in the master bedroom open onto a private deck and a magnificent view of the St. Croix River. Horizontal copper tube railing minimizes obstruction of the view. The arch is subtly recessed, as are the windows and trim.**

Left, top **Living and formal dining rooms are set two steps down from the kitchen/informal dining area, creating a clear boundary and distinction between the spaces. The floors are Brazilian cherry, chosen for its beauty and extraordinary durability—an important consideration in a home with active children.**

Left, bottom **A pair of broad stair landings are a favorite place for children to play. A built-in storage unit borders the stairs and holds games, books, and toys.**

Right **The stone fireplace and the exposed post-and-beam structure give a feeling of strength and durability to this area, a good balance to the transparency of the window-filled walls.**

and entertaining. A hallway on the opposite side of the kitchen leads to a quiet study, the laundry room, the mudroom, and a powder room.

The central kitchen opens directly onto a spacious breakfast nook, where an open stairway leads to the second-floor bedrooms. The kitchen/dining area is the most-used space in the house, and according to Tom and Dorothy, a parent standing at the kitchen island has visual access to most of the first floor and can keep an ear open for activities on the second floor.

The kitchen/dining area was designed to be a self-contained, highly functional, social space where everyone in the family feels at home. The full range of family activities takes place here, and the space serves as a mini-great room. The kitchen features counters on three sides and a central work island, a design that allows for family participation in meal preparation and cleanup. In the afternoons, the dining area is a favorite place for kids to do their homework, and the nearby open stairway's two landings are choice spots for play.

Michaela suggested that the Stormonts include a built-in padded bench—an unusual feature in a dining area—but everyone in the Stormont family uses and appreciates it. In the mornings, Mom and Dad enjoy sitting there with a cup of coffee and the newspaper; in the evenings, parents and children cuddle up for storytime; and just about anytime, the children take over this cozy alcove for card playing and board games.

Leaving the Dirt at the Door

The mudroom and the playroom are important spaces in the Stormont home. The mudroom features a cement floor, a utility tub, and lots of coat hooks placed at kid height. A pass-through into the kitchen allows a child on Rollerblades to skate into the mudroom, ask Mom or Dad in the kitchen to hand them whatever they need, and skate back outside without tracking up the house. "The whole idea is never to let the dirt inside in the first place," says Dorothy. "Who wants to be after their kids all the time?"

Just beyond the mudroom are the laundry room and a tiled bathroom with a stall shower. When a child comes in from soccer practice, swimming lessons, or digging a hole in the backyard, dirty, soggy clothing goes directly to the laundry room, and dirty, soggy children head for the shower.

A Room of Our Own

The playroom is on the second floor, conveniently close to the children's bedrooms. It's a large open space with a dramatically pitched ceiling and banks of windows on two walls for lots of natural light. The playroom is purposely plain, with plush wall-to-wall carpeting. It is the kind of neutral, open, safe space that can

Above *Low-hung hooks inside the mudroom door catch kids' coats and knapsacks. Cement makes a virtually maintenance-free floor surface. The step up leads to a tile hallway (also low maintenance) where the pass-through provides direct access to the kitchen.*

Opposite *The favorite seat in the house. This built-in bench is a cozy alcove in the kitchen/dining area. Built-in storage below is handy and unobtrusive.*

I t was a one-third-acre lot—spacious enough—but it was steeply sloped, it had a long, narrow drive that would require a space-consuming turn-around, and the local codes restricted the house to two bedrooms because of water limits. On the other hand, the views of the California coastline were great and so was the school district. "It was a site that only an architect with small children could love," declares Brian Cearnal.

The home that Brian designed here for his family does much more than simply solve the challenges posed by a difficult site, however. This is a quintessential family home, and its design is imbued with the values that Brian and his wife Judi are committed to instilling in their three young children. The home features Hispanic and Mediterranean-style elements, an echo of happy times that the couple spent together in Mexico. Within this framework, there is an easy flow from one room to the next, for spaces are meant to be shared and enjoyed. "There's no place here that's off-limits to the kids," says Judi. "Every room's a playroom!" For the Cearnals, the many light-hearted touches, the extensive use of bright colors, and the finely handcrafted materials used throughout the house all reflect the warmth of their family life and the exuberant high spirits of their children.

It's a Jungle Out There!

Inside and out, this is a home that is intended for a growing family, where the needs and interests of the children have been clearly addressed at every phase of the design process. Even the landscaping was planned to be part of the fun. Brian and Judi both

Above **A series of wall insets create a warm, human-scale entrance. Plants and climbing vines soften the courtyard, and the quarry tile floor continues into the entry, drawing the outside indoors.**

Opposite **The tile roof, wrought-iron details, warm colors, and simple forms are a natural fit for the coastal foothills of southern California. The epitome of a Mediterranean or Hispanic villa, it is a comfortable family home where the owners are raising three young children.**

Left, top **A composition of geometry—this view from the backyard fort to the kitchen shows the Hispanic roots of the home's design. Drought-resistant plants provide shade and privacy for the enclosed play yard.**

Left, bottom **There are no walls to separate the three kids who share this bedroom. The children are still young enough to thrive in a closely shared environment, and nighttime is family time as Mom or Dad sits in the rocker to read a bedtime story.**

Above **The unusual placement of the kitchen sink away from the outer wall allows parents to see out through the eating nook and keep an eye on the play yard. The central work island is offset from the kitchen's traffic flow, allowing parents and children to work together on meal preparation.**

grew up in a rural community where there were orchards to roam and lots of room to play, and they wanted their children to experience some of this, despite their new home's in-city location. The front hillside, known as "the jungle," is planted with avocado and citrus trees, and it features a sturdily built fort as well.

In addition to being a favorite play area, "the jungle" is a visual buffer that separates the Cearnal house from the street below and surrounds it with nature, something that both children and parents appreciate. By stacking the bedrooms over the living spaces, Brian was able to maximize the amount of level yard out back. Here the Cearnals have created a kid-friendly expanse of green lawn amid the otherwise drought-resistant plants. Access to the yard is through the kitchen eating nook (to facilitate quick pit stops for snacks) or down an unusually narrow stairway—scaled just for kids—that leads directly from the children's second-floor bedroom.

One for All and All for One

Bedroom. Singular. From the very beginning, the Cearnals had to accept the fact that their children would share a single bedroom. While most people are locked into the idea that each child should have his or her own room, the Cearnals note that many experts believe children don't necessarily want that much isolation. And their personal experience has borne this out, for the Cearnal kids are thriving in their close quarters. According to Judi and Brian, the large and airy shared bedroom has been a crucial element in developing tender, conciliatory sibling relationships.

The children's room has windows on two exterior walls and doors to the hallway on either end. "If the kids ever need it, we can partition the room right down the middle," says Judi. "Our 12-year-old is beginning to lobby for a little more privacy, for example. He may eventually take over the first-floor den as his bedroom, although he's not interested in being so far away just yet."

fter establishing their careers elsewhere, the owners of this house moved back to the Twin Cities area so they could raise their two young daughters near extended family. They purchased an older, modest home on a beautiful piece of suburban lakefront property. Although the house was inadequate for their needs, the location was perfect—and just minutes away from grandparents. The new homeowners considered an extensive renovation, but ultimately decided that to create the home they wanted for their family, the best alternative was to tear down the old house and rebuild on the foundation.

Northwoods Formal

The couple asked architect Robert Gerloff to help them create a home where they could raise their family and grow old together. They decided to extend themselves as far as they could financially and pay for their dreams over time. The house was to blend the casual ambiance of an old-fashioned Minnesota lake house with the sophisticated, urban tastes of the homeowners. The center of the house would be a well-integrated living space that took maximum advantage of the view. In addition to three family bedrooms that would share the second floor, a main floor space would double as a guest room and home office.

This home by the lake combines a rustic exterior of exposed logs and board-and-batten siding with a formal window layout and a highly detailed interior for a look that Robert calls "Northwoods formal." A spacious great hall integrates living, dining, and library spaces. The great hall is given definition by the use of archways that separate one "room" from the next. The library features a barrel-vaulted ceiling painted a dramatic dark blue and set with antique

Above **The shed-roof porch and horizontal board-and-batten siding give the house a relaxed, rustic look. Minimal windows on the street (north) side means more windows allotted to the sunny lake (south) side of the house.**

Right **Custom metal balusters and a curved landing step accent the arched passageway. The floorplan joins living, dining, and library spaces and opens them to the outside deck and the lake beyond. This is a design strategy that brings the outdoors into the core of the house.**

Left *In the library, a cozy reading area sits under a star-studded, barrel-coved "sky." What better place to read* Goodnight Moon *to a child before bedtime? High windows let in light while screening out the view of neighboring homes.*

Right **The informal eating area in the kitchen has a view of the fireplace, which is made of local rock. The arch detail above the fireplace mirrors the arch into the kitchen, integrating the theme of curves throughout the main floor.**

Opposite, top **The freestanding cabinet in the middle of an arched passageway acts as a visual buffer without entirely blocking the view or the light.**

Opposite, bottom **This kitchen island provides seating away from the room's main traffic flow. The yellow tile backsplash is bright, durable, and easy to clean. The bright red floor echoes the home's exterior.**

brass stars. The use of a few specially selected design elements sets the library corner of the great hall apart as the homeowners' retreat. At the owners' request, the kitchen is a bit removed from the living space. While adjacent to the great hall through a broad arched opening, the kitchen is visually separated by a large freestanding cabinet.

A Room with a Future

Beyond the fireplace in the living area, a professional home office doubles as a guest room. This space was planned for the long term. The homeowners wanted it to be a room where an aging parent might be comfortable for an extended stay. Or, in their own later years, the space could become a first-floor master suite for the couple.

According to Robert, the real challenge of designing homes for families is building options into the design. "People tend to see themselves as frozen in time, and the architect must bring a larger understanding of how a family changes through time," explains Robert. "The needs that a young couple can identify for themselves and their small children transform through time in ways that no one can foresee." A room as well positioned and flexible as this guest room/home office is a wonderful resource that can ease the pressures of family life.

Reconsidering the Home Office

The location of a home office is a very personal decision, especially when the office will receive a high level of use, as is the case here. During the planning stages, the owners asked for an office that was separate from—but close to—family life. In retrospect, they've found that the office space is a little too close to the action, especially when there's a pressing work deadline. The homeowners have plans to tear down and rebuild their old, freestanding garage, and they've asked Robert to include another home office as part of the new garage design.

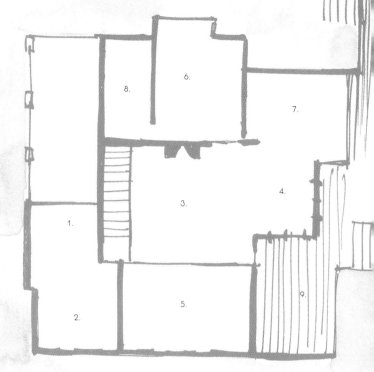

Relocating the home office to another building on the property will allow for a greater separation of work life from family life. At the same time, the uses for the current office/guest room will be expanded. It may someday become a quiet den where children can do their homework, or a teen bedroom. The creation of a second home office opens up the possibility that both spouses might someday work from home.

Together and Apart

Family bedrooms are on the second floor, all with views of the lake. The two children's rooms have almost the same amount of floor space, although the space in one of the bedrooms is divided into a bedroom and a play loft. The children share a bathroom they reach through a small anteroom with a vanity sink, a feature that should help keep bathroom skirmishes to a minimum—even when the homeowners' two daughters reach adolescence.

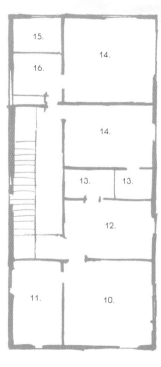

Upper Floor

10. Master Bedroom
11. Master Bath
12. Dressing Room/ "Insomnia" Room
13. Walk-in Closet (Play Loft above)
14. Bedroom
15. Bath
16. Washroom

Main Floor

1. Entry
2. Mudroom
3. Living Room
4. Dining Room
5. Kitchen
6. Home Office
7. Library
8. Bath
9. Deck

Right, top *This long stair landing doubles as the bedroom hallway. Windows face the street and bring in an abundance of diffuse, northern light.*

Right, bottom *A captain's ladder leads to the play loft. The unusually high chair rail allows a mix of colors—the dark blue gives this child's bedroom a feeling of coziness, while the white above helps disperse the light from the windows, making the small space feel larger.*

The master suite features a generously sized dressing area that doubles as an "insomnia room." If one spouse wants to stay up late to read, there's no need to go all the way downstairs to avoid disturbing the other. A small television in the insomnia room makes late-night television viewing convenient but separate from the bedroom.

There are many spaces in this house for the family to be together, as well as spaces especially for parents (the insomnia room) and the children. The basement level is primarily the domain of the children. A large dedicated playroom and hobby space shares the lower level with a sauna and the laundry room. According to the homeowners, their daughters spend a lot of time playing down here. This is the most casual part of the house, where the children can set up their toys and really spread out. As their girls get older, the homeowners foresee that this playroom will continue to serve as a rec room and teen retreat.

Above **The slate floor of the entry is warm, earthy, and virtually indestructible. Built-in cupboards hold outdoor gear and double as a window seat and shoe-changing bench. The large windows capture the north light for the entry and the living area beyond.**

Opposite **The deck winds its way toward a small, summer house—a free-standing screen porch. The white columns are a formal contrast to the Northwoods look and hint at the sophisticated interior.**

the complexities of keeping it simple

According to architect Robert Gerloff, as the demand for urban and suburban living space becomes increasingly tight, tear-downs will become more and more common. "It makes a lot of sense to rebuild on an existing foundation," says Robert. "The challenge of a tear-down is in all the quirks you inherit from the old foundation." The sawtooth footprint that creates the elegant great hall of this lakefront home is the direct descendant of three separate room additions to the original house. "You don't see the amount of work that goes into making something look simple," says Robert. "Sometimes, it can be very difficult to get it all to resolve nicely."

Bob and Judy are "empty nesters" who consider themselves anything but. Yes, their six children are grown and they are doting grandparents five times over, and yes, they are active people who lead busy lives. But Bob and Judy are in their true element when they're serving up bountiful family meals, surrounded by their kids and grandkids. The most important request they made of architect Jon Anderson was that their new home in Albuquerque, New Mexico, become family headquarters—the place where everyone would come together for holidays, family celebrations, Sunday dinners, or for the very best of all possible reasons, no special reason at all.

Full Bloom
in the Desert

While family was the top priority, the house needed to fulfill other important functions, as well. Friends and associates were to be made welcome at frequent social gatherings, business meetings, and charitable events, so the house had to reflect Bob and Judy's personalities, their sense of beauty, and their gracious, Southwestern hospitality. The couple are contractors who specialize in fine, one-of-a-kind, architect-designed homes, so in addition to the usual complement of public rooms, they required a hard-working home office. And with so much volume and variety of activities based in the house, they wanted a quiet retreat for themselves where they could relax at the end of a busy day.

Dinner Is Served

As the pace of modern life continues to accelerate, people are realizing that true happiness depends on the ability to focus clearly on personal priorities, not only in their lives, but in their homes as well. In Bob and Judy's case, this meant spending more time at

Above **Inset glass blocks let light into the living room and echo lattice partitions at the home's entry.**

Right **In the hot Albuquerque climate, this blue-tiled fountain creates a cool and inviting entry. The central dining hall is a brightly hued celebration of a room where family and friends gather to break bread and share good times.**

home and putting out a large and loving welcome mat for their close-knit family. Five of their six adult children and their families live in the Albuquerque area, and all are frequent guests. "The kids all have their own keys to our house," reports Judy. "They drop by sometimes just to see what's in the fridge—we think it's great!" And because dinnertime has been the centerpiece of this family's life since the old days when the kids still lived at home, it was almost inevitable that the sharing of meals would become the major theme of Bob and Judy's new house.

At the very heart of the home is the dining room, a spacious hall that also serves as the main entryway from the outside world. Despite its vibrantly colored walls, blue tile floor detail (which continues into outside fountains), and expansive windows and doorways to every other part of the house, the dining room is actually very spare. It was carefully composed to contain only those objects that Judy and Bob most value, an approach that befits the most important room in the house. The dining table was especially designed for the hall and comfortably seats 14—Judy, Bob, their six children, and their children's spouses and partners. A treasured Colombian nativity is displayed in the dining room's "nicho" (or niche), a place of honor that it has held in all of Bob and Judy's homes. "I've had nichos in all our houses," explains Judy. "I leave the nativity out all year long and decorate it with votive candles."

Rooms That Work Overtime

Just off the dining room, the kitchen is completely open to a large family area, where a handmade trestle table and benches offer an informal setting for casual meals and an out-of-the way perch for family and friends to gather while Judy is cooking. A hallway off the living room leads to the guest wing,

Opposite, top **The dining room is a spacious central hall entryway and the home's true center. Rooms and hallways radiate from this center like side streets.**

Opposite, bottom **This rustic, knotty-pine trestle table recalls the owners' Hispanic roots and stands in counterpoint to the sophisticated, refined cabinet work of the kitchen. The fireplace is open to both the kitchen and the dining room.**

Right **Building materials were selected to keep things cool. Glass blocks on the southern wall let in light but keep out heat. In contrast to its one magenta wall, the rest of the living room is monochromatic. The wood ceiling brings in another layer of natural materials.**

n 1986, architect Mac Godley's brother Rick asked him to design a home. More than anything else, Rick wanted a place where he could rest, relax, and really unwind from his busy career in New Haven. Mac located the perfect piece of property for Rick's refuge—two acres on the Connecticut shore with views across the salt marshes to Long Island Sound.

As plans for the new house began to take shape, Rick proposed that his brother Mac join him and share the house once it was built. The design evolved to provide each brother with an identical, independent master suite set under a pair of matching gable rooflines. Below the bedrooms, a shared living room and library opened onto expansive decks that were oriented to take in the view. Mac and Rick lived comfortably in their shared home for several years until changes in each of their lives called for changes in their living arrangements. Ultimately, the house was put up for sale.

A Tale of Two Families

In 1997, single dad Bill Kirwin and his high-school-age daughter Lindsay were living in a cookie-cutter neocolonial in the suburbs. On weekends, they liked to tour very expensive, very contemporary houses for sale. They weren't seriously looking to buy one of these multimillion dollar mansions. Rather, Lindsay was interested in pursuing a career in architecture, and these outings were a fun and educational way of spending time together. Inevitably, one day a real estate agent called Bill to say that a very interesting, very contemporary

Above **A widow's walk offers a sweeping view of the tranquil marshlands that border the house.**

Right **Mirror-image stairways lead from the family entry to two independent master suites on the second floor. The central skylight brings light into the center of the house. Custom built-in planter boxes upstairs provide a refreshing touch of green.**

home was just coming on the market—and this one was within his price range. Best of all, the home was perfect for a single father and his almost-grown daughter. In addition to comfortable living room, library, kitchen, and beautiful view decks, the home featured two identical, independent master suites set under matching gable rooflines.

Seeing Double

Even on the outside, the theme of separate but equal is apparent in this house. Twin gables over separate garages frame the central family entrance (a less-used, formal entrance is around the corner). Once inside, a pair of staircases lead to separate balconies, where twin master bedrooms, bathrooms, and guest rooms are mirror images of each other. A walkway between the two balconies allows for visiting.

Each spacious master bedroom features peaked ceilings, open loft spaces, and built-in window seats. Large walk-in closets, one for each master suite, line the common wall to maximize sound insulation between the spaces. Outer doors in each room open to a large, shared second-floor deck. Open rafters above the deck extend the line of the roof gables and filter the sunlight during the warmest part of the day. When the house was first built, the Godley brothers used their guest rooms to extend their living/working spaces, and house guests were put up in the first floor library. Today, Bill has set up "his" guest room as a home office, while the spare room on Lindsay's side of the house is used as the family guest room.

Coming Together

On the main floor, a central atrium opens to the communal spaces, with doorways leading to the living/dining room,

Opposite *Each of the two master bedrooms is a private space set apart from the rest of the house. Daybeds top built-in storage, and French doors open onto the second-floor deck.*

Right *French doors can close off the entry hallway from the living area to control heat and give privacy. To keep the doors out of the way—and make them almost disappear—the hallway walls are recessed to enclose the fully opened doors.*

library, and kitchen. The large living/dining room extends across the front of the house to take in the view. Just outside, a large hot tub sits in a private alcove, and a series of decks expands the home's living space and sees a great deal of use throughout the seasons. In addition to the main-floor and second-floor decks, a third-story widow's walk is nestled in the dual rooflines.

The living room gets more use than any other room in the house. Clerestory windows here throw natural light onto the wood ceiling,

which brightens and lightens the space. The carefully framed views of the shoreline provide an ever-changing natural backdrop. According to Bill, this is an extremely comfortable space to be in, whether alone, with his daughter, or with a roomful of friends. The kitchen is three steps up from the living area, a strategy that provides the cook with great sight lines to the view. A recessed door and a large *shoji* screen can be closed to hide kitchen clutter. The library is a quiet, first-floor retreat for reading, watching television, or surfing the Net.

Above *Three steps lead up to the kitchen, which provides added visual separation from the dining area. Cupboards are placed unusually high on the wall to allow for a bank of windows above the kitchen counters.*

Opposite *A wall of windows provides a backdrop of views in the living/dining room. Light-colored carpeting contrasts with the wood ceilings and reflects extra light into the room.*

Below *The comfortable library features built-in shelving and rich wood storage cabinets. The computer desk sits unobtrusively in a corner alcove.*

The Daughter Dynamic

Providing adequate—and appropriate—spaces for children is a crucial factor in establishing a comfortable, enjoyable family life. "More and more, fathers are getting custody of their children," says Bill. "Particularly when it's a father/daughter relationship, it creates a different dynamic. One of the things this house expresses for us is that dynamic." While the house was originally conceived and built so that adult siblings could lead independent lives, it functions exceptionally well for the Kirwins as their family home. The bilateral second-floor design provides Lindsay with the privacy and independence she needs as a young adult, while allowing father and daughter to remain together as a family.

"Dreaming up this house was collaborative, a real family effort—we talked about it for years," says Frank Doherty of the home he shares with his wife Janice and their two teenage daughters. For much of their married life, the Dohertys lived wherever the demands of Frank's career as an airline pilot dictated. When they were finally in a position to plan their next move for themselves, Frank and Janice were ready to come to a place where they could build the home of their dreams and settle in for the long haul. "It was important for everybody to feel good about what we were doing," Frank continues, "so everybody got their say."

Fly Away Home

Frank and Janice wanted the center of their new home to be an elegantly furnished formal dining room that flowed into a secluded sitting room. These rooms were to be the family's inner

sanctum, far away from the noise and bustle of the rest of the house. They wanted an informal family room that would open onto a spacious, comfortable kitchen where Janice could cook and Frank could bake without getting in each other's way. They wanted an old-fashioned butler's pantry, a feature they had loved in a former house, a place where they could display their collections of china, glass, and silver.

The Doherty daughters wanted private bedrooms and adequate bathroom space, but what they really lobbied for was an old-fashioned wraparound covered porch. Everyone wanted the house to honor their sense of beauty by incorporating elements of the Victorian and Arts and Crafts styles that they all loved.

Above **The house commands the highest spot on the property with views to the gardens and beyond. Craftsman elements like the exposed rafter tails, small windows, and generous overhangs create a feeling of compact sturdiness for an enduring family home.**

Right **A center peninsula separates the kitchen into dual work stations, a design that solves the problem of multiple cooks in a limited space. The custom cherry wood cabinets complement the owners' collection of antique green glassware.**

Main Floor

1. Entry
2. Sitting Room
3. Dining Room
4. Kitchen
5. Pantry
6. Bath
7. Family Room
8. Eating Nook
9. Porch

Opposite **Exposed beams
are a familiar Arts and Crafts
detail. The heavy timbers
of the gabled entrance
reinforce the sense that
this house is substantial
and secure.**

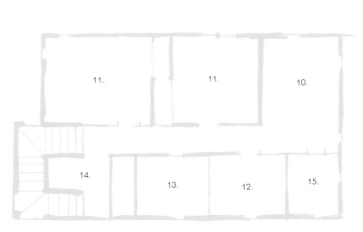

Upper Floor

10. Master Bedroom
11. Bedroom
12. Master Bath
13. Bath
14. Laundry
15. Closet

Quality over Quantity

Homeowners typically engage an architect to translate their family's needs into a design that will meet those needs, but the Dohertys came to builder/architect Andy Reese with a definite program in hand for a design they wanted him to refine and execute. Reese was the right man for the job. He believes in using his knowledge of architecture as a service to fulfill his clients' goals—not to lay on them his ideas. "Discourse and drawings bring the dreams to life," remarks Andy. The home he realized for the Dohertys is Victorian in form, with Craftsman bungalow interior detailing and a wraparound porch, all oriented to capture the view.

As is the case for most families, the Dohertys had to scale back on some of their dreams so that the house would fit their budget. Ultimately, they decided to sacrifice additional living space in order to gain a particularly high level of craftsmanship. The choice of quality over quantity is an increasingly common one—a strategy that balances the budget while allowing for the fine details that imbue a home with personal meaning. Janice and Frank worked with Reese from the inside out so that the design of their home would beautifully frame their collections of beloved fixtures and furnishings. For example, there was no need to buy lighting fixtures. "All the lighting fixtures in the house are antiques," explains Frank. "We had been collecting them for years."

The Dohertys took an equally active role in the construction of their home. While the house was being built, Frank spent every free moment working side by side with Andy and his crew. Janice and the girls did much of the finishing and later on made everything from lampshades to lace curtains. The family's hands-on involvement was about a lot more than saving money. This is a home that the whole clan had a hand in creating, and everywhere they look they can see the fruits of their own labor. They all agree that this elegant little house has already become the Dohertys' ancestral home.

Above *A Craftsman-era stained-glass window lowers the hallway at the entrance to the kitchen and creates a subtle but distinct delineation between the formal and informal regions of the home.*

Opposite *The wraparound porch leads from the front door to the pantry entrance and borders the gardens that encircle the house. The diamond-shaped pattern stained on the decking breaks up the expanse and gives it an appealing visual texture.*

A World Apart

Time together takes on special meaning for an airline pilot's family. "When Frank leaves for work in the morning, it's not like he's going to be home at five o'clock the same evening," says Janice. Typically, Frank is away from home for half of each week. When he is at home, the center of family life is dinner in the formal dining room followed by quiet conversation in the adjoining parlor.

Rather than creating the open environment of a great room, where there is an easy flow from one activity to the next, the Dohertys very consciously created their formal dining room and parlor as a world apart. The rooms are acoustically and aesthetically distinct from the kitchen/family room, and they represent a separate realm where family members can focus their attention on one another.

Everything about the dining room and parlor sets the space apart, and the house has been expressly designed to keep these spaces separate. Rooms are sited and walls placed so that there is no visual access from the formal rooms into the more informal kitchen and family room. The lack of sight lines suits the Dohertys because it reinforces their original decision to leave the rest of the world outside for a few hours a day and spend quality time together as a family.

History in the Making

There is an especially telling detail in the Doherty home, although it is not apparent to the naked eye. In one of the tapered columns that separate the sitting and dining rooms, there's a steel time capsule that contains personal notes, photos, and plans that document the creation of the home—the history of the family built into the very structure of the house. The exact location is a secret shared only by family members, and they intend to pass the secret on to future generations.

Above **Warmed by an enameled stove, the casual dining area is bathed in natural light. The family room alcove is tucked out of the way. The television is carefully placed to minimize its intrusion into the larger space.**

Opposite **A coffered ceiling, elegant light fixtures, antique furniture, a plate rail, and classic cabbage rose wallpaper create a formal space dedicated to fine dining and family togetherness. The formal parlor beyond provides an intimate retreat for conversation far away from the bustle of the kitchen and family room.**

n 1989, architect Scott Rappe bought a century-old "four-flat" in East Village, one of Chicago's oldest neighborhoods. Scott, a fourth-generation Chicagoan, transformed the four apartments into two spacious rental units and renovated the unfinished third-floor attic into an open, loft-style apartment for himself.

In 1993, Scott married architect Grace Kuklinski. The newlyweds wanted a little more living space, so in 1994 they opened and closed a few passageways and transformed the back half of the second-floor apartment into a master bedroom for themselves. Late in 1996, Grace and Scott became parents. Shortly after that, they said goodbye to the tenants who occupied the second-floor front apartment, opened up the entire space, and expanded their apartment to include a family room and a nursery for their infant son. Over the years, what Scott and Grace have found here is a flexibility that allows them to transform their home as their needs and requirements change.

The Many Lives of a Four-Flat

Loft Life

The main part of the Rappe home is the original third-floor loft set under the steeply pitched roofline. Scott installed a series of dormers and cross gables during the 1989 renovation to expand the volume of space and bring natural light into the loft. At one end, the living area features an exposed brick wall and the building's old—and tilted—central chimney. These century-old architectural elements stand in contrast to the Rappe's contemporary furniture and the sleek, white cabinets in the kitchen/dining area. The flooring here is seconds of ash, a cost-conscious

Right **At first glance, this is a typical, old-style Chicago brick row house. The only evidence of the extensive renovation of the attic space is the new dormers visible on the roof. The renters' entrance is visible on the right, while the owners' primary entrance is through the wrought-iron gate to the left of the house.**

Above **Though small, this office is more than adequate. The unadorned work station is all business, while leaded-glass cupboard doors add visual interest and extra storage space.**

Left, top **The renovation kept the living area's attic roofline intact, while small dormer windows bring in light. The Adirondack chair chronicles the family's Chicago history, painted with many visual references to the neighborhood.**

Left, bottom **Canvas insets create a childproof railing. Books remain clean, organized—and out of little hands—behind glass doors.**

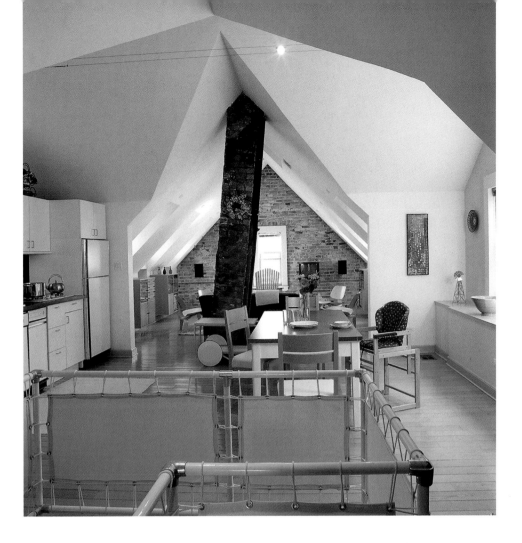

choice. It was stained in two different colors, which adds texture and visual interest to the loft. Six small dormers in the living area bring light directly into the room, and niches under each dormer window display the couple's collection of pottery and glassware.

Although neither Grace nor Scott work full time at home, a shared office on the third floor sees a lot of action in the evenings after their son goes to bed. The office door is set in a partial wall, a strategy that allows the Rappes to close off the space without losing the light from the office's windows. An interior window keeps the office connected to the rest of the loft even when the door is closed. A pair of compact, L-shaped work stations gives each spouse a place to work undisturbed. Just outside the office door, glassed-in bookshelves provide additional storage.

Right **Dormers and cross-gables expanded a cramped attic into this spacious, light-filled loft. And yes, the chimney does lean. The owner-architect's theory: It was made this way on purpose to prevent back drafts.**

Bedding Down

Bedrooms and family room are one flight down. "There hasn't been a great deal of physical reconstruction here," says Scott. "When we took over the second floor we changed the names of rooms more than changing their sizes or shapes." The second floor still has a small kitchen, for example, a remnant of its last incarnation as a separate apartment. Grace and Scott simply used the kitchen counter as the changing table for their baby. And having a place just off the family room where they can store cold drinks or heat up the kettle for tea saves on trips upstairs to the main kitchen.

A small room off the nursery has been transformed into their son's library. "It's really like a big walk-in closet with a window," explains Grace. "We made it into a quiet space reserved for books. We read to him in there, and he goes in there by himself sometimes to be alone. It's really his space."

Quick-Change Architecture

The hallmark of this home is its ability to change with the times. According to Scott and Grace, it is precisely because the building was built as a speculative four-flat for no particular client that it survives as a model of adaptability. The original design featured stairs at the front and middle of the building, as well as a plan that divided the flats into zones of narrow rooms and wide rooms. "Our renovation design exploits the inherent flexibility of these original design features and establishes a variety of areas within the building that can be linked together as the needs of our family change," explains Scott.

Why not just sell the place and move out to a single-family dwelling in the suburbs? Quite simply, the Rappes love living in the city. "Scott's office is one block away from our house, and my office is a 15-minute commute on public transportation," notes Grace. The

Above **Small, enclosed spaces make comfortable hideaways that children can use and enjoy. This tiny room off the nursery was formerly a closet.**

Opposite **The second-floor nursery is open to the family room. The built-in, used to store children's books, games, and toys, is the original china hutch in the kitchen of this 1892 apartment.**

The owners of this house wanted to raise their two young daughters in a low-key, rural environment, so they moved their family from San Francisco to the Sonoma Valley. They rented a comfortable house while they looked for a home to buy. Instead of finding the perfect house, however, they found the perfect piece of property—four-plus acres with a view across the valley, a seasonal creek, and a huge, old ash tree. The owners envisioned a rambling, single-story home where they could spread out and raise their family, a place that would be as lovely as the idyllic setting. They approached architect Andy Neumann, a friend of the family, and asked him to design a wine-country farmhouse in his informal, yet elegant style.

The New Family
Farmhouse

The couple explained to Andy that they wanted a lot out of their new home. It was to be a place where they could live in harmony with the seasons, but they were looking for strategies to keep the mud, dust, and the bugs outside, too. They wanted a home that would be comfortable and easy to maintain, but beautifully finished with fine detail work and well-chosen materials. They wanted kid-friendly spaces and a casual, open kitchen/family room for everyday living, but also a separate formal living room, dining room, and library. Andy assured them that all of these disparate elements could be integrated into their new family home.

Making Places by Balancing Spaces

Homes need to afford adequate privacy for individuals, provide zones where family members can all gather together, as well as make room for visits from family and friends. Often, a single space in a home will address multiple purposes. Here, however, Andy's

Above **The rural architecture of Sonoma County, California, is captured with white clapboard siding, a green asphalt shingle roof, and a generous wraparound porch.**

Right **The gabled ceiling enhances the feeling that the master bedroom is a separate structure and a place all its own, an intimate retreat for the homeowners. French doors open to a private deck and the view of the surrounding fields.**

design carefully balances separate individual, family, and guest spaces, with approximately one-third of the home's square footage apportioned to each type.

The home is built around a large central entry, with hallways leading to the kitchen/family room wing, the bedroom wing, and the formal wing, which is composed of a living room, a dining room, and a library. A butler's pantry provides access directly between the kitchen and the dining room, but for the most part, it's necessary to pass through the central entry to go from one part of the house to another.

The homeowners use and enjoy every part of their home, and despite the apparent formality, the family enjoys a relatively informal lifestyle. The living and dining rooms are favorites for entertaining guests, but they are used by the family as well. The living room is a favorite spot for a little quiet time, and the family eats a sit-down dinner together in the formal dining room several evenings a week.

Working the Room

The kitchen/family room wing is the most-used part of the house. The center of the kitchen is a large, granite-topped work island with an eating bar. As in many family kitchens, this is a favorite spot for afternoon snacks, homework, and visiting with the cook. The family room features a cozy window seat, a sunny dining alcove, and a floor-to-ceiling, river-rock fireplace. On very special family occasions like Valentine's Day, the family room is rearranged and the dining table is set up directly in front of the fireplace.

An old-fashioned screen porch, where the family dines and relaxes during the warm summer months, is used primarily as a mudroom the rest of the year; the owners would like to find a better use for this space. They plan to put up (removable) glass panels so that the screen porch can be used year-round as a teen retreat. Perfectly positioned for this use, the screen porch is visually isolated and somewhat removed from the family room. At the same time, it's close enough to the kitchen/family room to allow for discreet parental supervision.

Opposite, top **White-painted beaded ceiling, trusses, walls, and cabinetwork give the kitchen/family room an airy, casual appearance and contrast with the warm finish of the maple floor. The large cooking island features a second sink, a real convenience in any family kitchen.**

Opposite, bottom **Dad's study. The library features floor-to-ceiling bookshelves, dark-colored woodwork, and heavy, masculine furniture. The room has its own feeling, different and distinct from the rest of the house. This is a place for retreat, reflection, and study.**

Right **The formal living room has the warm colors and cozy feel of a country home. Furniture is arranged for comfort and conversation, and a wicker armchair adds a distinctly informal note.**

A Private Space

The bedroom wing is a quiet refuge from activities in other parts of the house. Each of the homeowners' daughters has an identical bedroom, complete with a built-in window seat, armoire, and desk. When designing bedrooms for children, it is important either to give each child a specially chosen bedroom feature or, as the homeowners have done here, to give each child an identical, relatively neutral room that can be personalized and individualized.

The two bedrooms share a common bathroom, where each girl has her own sink, counter space, and mirror. Usually, children's bathrooms are placed along a bedroom hallway, and the children share a single, common bathroom door. In this house, a door in each child's bedroom leads into their bathroom. There's a third door in the bathroom, but rather than leading back into the bedroom hallway, it opens directly to the yard outside. The master bathroom has outdoor access as well. After an afternoon playing in the yard, digging in the garden, or taking a dip in the pool, family members come directly to their bathrooms where they can shed dirty clothes or wet bathing suits and clean up.

Double doors in the entry can be closed to give the bedroom wing a greater sense of privacy. The bedroom hallway is unusually wide. One wall features built-in shelves and cabinets for books, family photos, television and video equipment. On the opposite wall, a cozy built-in window seat sits in a well-lit alcove (see the photo on p. 2). Further along the wall, display rails feature an ever-changing exhibit of kid art. Like the family room on the opposite side of the house, this is a casual space where family members can relax with their feet up, watch a little television, and unwind. Unlike the family room, it is a very private space, intended primarily for family members. According to the homeowners, their daughters can sometimes be found curled up together here at bedtime.

Above **The girls' bathroom features identical sinks, counter space, and mirrors. Transom windows above the bathtub let light into the water closet.**

Opposite **Each of the children's bedrooms features a built-in window seat. The architect interviewed the owners' older daughter (then age 5) by having her draw a picture of her new bedroom. She drew a window seat, and he honored her request.**

16.

17.

Left, top *The alcove inside the doorway to the master suite was designed to accommodate this antique tansu chest. The owners had requested a place of honor for this family heirloom.*

Left, bottom *The master bathroom features a whirlpool tub and a large shower. The clear-glass shower enclosure makes the room feel larger.*

Main Floor

1. Entry
2. Living Room
3. Kitchen
4. Dining Room
5. Family Room
6. Library
7. Powder Room
8. Butler's Pantry
9. Wine Cellar
10. Laundry
11. Screen Porch
12. Breakfast Nook
13. Pantry
14. Bedroom
15. Bath
16. Master Bedroom
17. Master Bath

Right *Screen porch and French doors serve as informal entries to the house. The wraparound porch allows the homeowners to follow either the sun or the shade throughout the day. The ancient ash tree is one of the things that drew the homeowners to this piece of land.*

Carl Berg and Judy Green Berg live in New York City, where they lead busy, professional lives. Their children are grown and out on their own. But when these empty nesters approached architect Jeremiah Eck to design a weekend place for them in the Berkshires, what they asked for was the very essence of a new family home.

They wanted it to be a second home for the two of them, as well as a place that could become their primary residence when they reach their retirement years. But more important, their new home was to be a place to share with their grown children and their aging parents. Life here was to be

The Weekend Family Home

about the joys and pleasures of the family—the sharing of good times and good food in a place where everyone could relax and renew themselves. They wanted an open, integrated living space for family gatherings and comfortably sized bedrooms for privacy and retreat. They asked that the home take advantage of the incomparable view of the sun setting over the Catskills, and they requested an open cooking hearth.

The view of the sunset and a family hearth were to become the central features of the Bergs' new home. With full views to the east, south, and west, Jeremiah designed the house around the idea of connecting people inside the house to the view outside. A large, sheltering roof was to encompass multi-use spaces, and a massive chimney would anchor the home to the site. At their first design meeting, Jeremiah showed Judy and Carl a tiny model—an umbrella supported by a sturdy chimney sitting on a broad platform. They were delighted with his vision for their new home.

Above **The soaring chimney anchors the roof to the core of the living space and serves as a backdrop to a cozy sitting area.**

Right **The screen porch is a transitional place, not quite indoors, not quite outdoors. The screened windows echo the main windows of the house.**

Left, top **A band of windows wraps around the living area and brings the surrounding countryside right inside. The posts, beams, and knee braces of the vaulted ceiling are painted white, defining the bones of the house.**

Left, bottom **The kitchen faces the rest of the living spaces, all of which share a central working hearth. Glass shelves and doors give the unit a feeling of lightness and diminish the scale of the upper cupboard. The poured-concrete counters match the hearth.**

Above **A variety of outdoor spaces share the platform deck that encircles the house. Broad steps frame the deck and give instant access to the lawn from anywhere on the platform.**

Right **The large central hearth serves three separate fireplaces and provides storage for wood. A wood grill faces the kitchen and is frequently used for cooking. The freestanding wood stove faces the dining area. The integral mantle ties the many facets of the chimney together.**

The Heart of the Home

The perimeter of the two-story great room is lined with windows that flood the space with light and provide views to the horizon in three directions. Although it is technically a single room, the kitchen and dining areas are set apart in their own alcoves. It is a comfortable room in which family and friends can be engaged in a variety of activities all at the same time.

The sense that there are several distinct areas here is enhanced by the imposing chimney. Set at the very center of the space, the chimney is shared by three separate fireplaces. In the kitchen, an open wood grill is an everyday cooking appliance. In the dining area, a wood stove sits at a diagonal under a high mantle. Easy chairs flank the living room's screened fireplace, a favorite spot to relax and visit or read a book.

There are a wide variety of places to gather, sit, and eat both inside and outside the Bergs' great room. French doors open onto the screen porch and the expansive decks, which are in almost constant use during the summer months. Jeremiah likes to think in terms of public versus private and formal versus informal. He believes that by getting away from outmoded ideas like "parlor" or "entry hall," living areas are more flexible and better able to respond to the needs of homeowners. For example, the Bergs initially asked for both formal and informal dining areas. Once they moved in, however, they realized that one dining area was adequate. The alcove just off the living area that was originally planned as a formal dining space is now the music area—the perfect spot for the Bergs' piano.

Family Bedrooms

Carl and Judy needed private space on the first floor that was acoustically and visually separate from the great room. This extra room serves a variety of purposes: it's a quiet den, office space for Carl, or a bedroom for Judy or Carl's mother when either comes to stay. The room is beautifully finished and quite spacious, and the Bergs could certainly use it as their own bedroom if age or infirmity ever make it difficult for them to use their second-floor master bedroom.

It was extremely important to Judy and Carl that their two grown children think of this new home as their home, so they each have their own bedroom here. "This is their home, too," says Carl. "They don't need an invitation." The three family bedrooms share a second "sleeping" floor that's reached by a common balcony.

Placing family bedrooms together keeps parents nearby and accessible for young children. However, with older teenagers or adult children, acoustic distance and separation are more important considerations. While the design of the Berg house dictated a central location for family bedrooms, Jeremiah positioned them so that they share no common walls and are actually quite separate. Bedroom doors are spaced well apart from each other on the balcony as well, so no one has to infringe on anyone else's space to get to their own room.

Open by Day, Cozy by Night

After their busy work weeks in the city, Carl and Judy are ready for the quiet and slower pace that is waiting for them at their home in the country, and they are happiest when they're sharing it with family. According to Carl, the house has an almost magical way of

Above **The unusual angle of this window wall projects the second-floor master bedroom toward the canopy of trees. The owners liken it to the prow of a ship.**

Opposite **The dining area sits in an alcove near the kitchen and opens onto a trellis-covered deck. A single Arts and Crafts–style hanging fixture lights the area.**

Below **The family bedrooms share this spacious balcony, which overlooks the living areas below. The unique design of the balustrade adds a playful, architectural touch.**

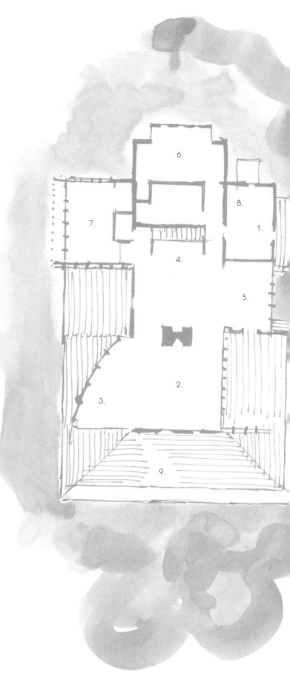

opening itself up during the day to encompass the view. "It's intensely visual here—this is what we wanted, something quite open that really lends itself to the setting," he explains. "And then at night, the walls reestablish themselves around us and it's a very cozy home."

Left **The trellis allows plenty of light to reach this section of the porch. Vines will eventually cover the trellis, which will filter the light in the summer. What better place for an afternoon nap?**

Main Floor

1. Entry
2. Living Hall
3. Music Room
4. Kitchen
5. Dining Room
6. Study
7. Screen Porch
8. Mudroom
9. Porch

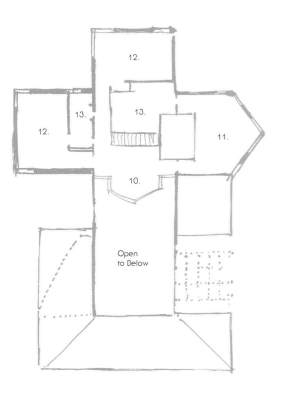

Open
to Below

Upper Floor

10. Balcony
11. Master Bedroom
12. Bedroom
13. Bath

from living room to living hall

"Over the past 50 years, American houses have become less formal. Formal spaces that I grew up in such as the living room have atrophied, while informal spaces such as the kitchen have become the center of activity in many houses.

"The Berg house is actually one continuous space consisting of kitchen and various dining/sitting situations. In fact, including the various options on the outside deck, there are seven spaces where one can sit or eat even though all the spaces are open to each other. The roof acts as an umbrella to all those spaces, while the chimney serves as a central reference.

"I call it the Living Hall house because the notion of a hall (much like the medieval hall) denotes a very open, informal plan around which most activity occurs."

—*Jeremiah Eck, architect*

Twenty years ago, Enrico and Nadia Natali purchased a private enclave of 40 pristine acres within the Los Padres National Forest near Ojai, California. It was a place of rare natural beauty, where the stars in the night sky were brilliant overhead and the sound of the wind in the trees was all they could hear. They named it Blue Heron Ranch for the majestic birds that they found there.

The property was secluded, down a rough dirt track five miles from the nearest paved road. There were no utilities or services of any kind to be had—no electricity, no running water, no telephone— and the nearest neighbor was a mile away. It was going to be an enormous challenge to create a home literally in the wilderness, but the place was well suited to their goal of unplugging themselves from the grid and becoming truly independent.

The Natalis planned to clear their own land, build their own home, grow their own gardens, and homeschool their three small children. Their dream of independent living has been refined over two decades of hands-on experience, and today the Natalis' home is an extensive complex surrounding a central courtyard.

A Modest Beginning

For the first few years, the land dictated Enrico and Nadia's living situation. Before they could build anything, they had to clear the thick chaparral that covered their property, and their first home was a large canvas tepee. "Knowing that it wasn't going to be forever is what actually made it okay—and we were really cozy there," remembers Nadia. Later on, when they began working on the plans for their house, the couple paid careful attention to the lessons they

Above **Solar panels on the roof help power this simple home, nestled in the Los Padres wilderness. The river rock used for walls, foundations, pathways, and terraces throughout the property was "harvested" from the land.**

Right **The central fireplace is the hearth, heart, and history of the family. Conceived as an intimate gathering place, the circle of broad steps is a comfortable perch where family and friends come together for conversation and contemplation.**

Blue Heron Ranch

Opposite, top **The simple, uncluttered great room is the center of family activity, from waking to sleeping. Stairs lead to the open bedroom loft, which runs the perimeter of the room.**

Opposite, bottom **Potted trees and plants are clustered near the expansive south-facing windows, blurring the separation between inside and out. Large clay tiles absorb the heat of the low winter sun, while the porch's broad overhang keeps them in the shade during the summer.**

Right **The main house and guest quarters frame a central courtyard, creating a serene and shaded environment. Paths lead up to and away from a large stone fountain. In the foreground, the massively built stone meditation house is an anchor to the rest of the compound.**

had learned from living in such intimate quarters. "We had to wonder why people had all of these little boxes to go sleep in," says Enrico. "If we got rid of them, we could have more room for living."

The Hearth of the Matter

The home that the Natalis built for themselves is small, simple, and beautifully handcrafted. A water pump provides them with running water from their own well, and generators furnish the electricity that allows for all the conveniences found in any modern house. But this home has much in common with family homes from a pre-industrial time as well. Back in the days when people were more closely tied to the land, resources were carefully guarded and all of a family's activities might revolve around a single hearth—as they do here.

Small and compact, the Natalis' home is a great room focused around a central wood stove that is set in a step-down hearth—the direct descendant of their tepee's central firepit. The compact kitchen forms an "L" along the eastern wall, and furniture is low to the ground and minimal. A flight of stairs leads to a communal sleeping loft, which lines two walls. The bathroom, the pantry, and a small den are tucked under the sleeping loft, but essentially, the Natali home is one spacious room.

This is the definitive expression of the great room concept, the place where everyone in the family co-exists. "When the children were very young, we had a line-up of beds upstairs, and that's where we all slept. It suited everybody's needs to be together," says Nadia. Inevitably, the toddlers who once held onto their parents' knees grew older and started needing more space and more privacy.

Over the years, the sleeping loft has seen all kinds of arrangements, with shelves and partitions used to carve out individual spaces to suit the needs of growing children. The first-floor den was ultimately appropriated and transformed into a private bedroom, first by the oldest Natali child and later on by each of the younger kids. Eventually, a small cabin, known as the Treehouse, was erected nearby for the ultimate in adolescent separation.

Building Dreams of Wood and Stone

Where once a single room was the center of all family activity, today the many separate buildings serve a variety of purposes. In addition to the original house and the Treehouse, Blue Heron Ranch has expanded to include a dining pavilion, a meditation house, a yurt, a guest trailer, a barn, and Enrico's workshop. While each building is unique, both in function and appearance, there is an overall cohesiveness to the compound. Porches extend living spaces and deep roof overhangs offer protection from the weather. Rock foundations and walls are massive and enduring. Naturally finished wood siding suits the country setting while revealing the careful craftsmanship and straightforward designs. Stone pathways connect the buildings to each other and create appealing patterns in the central courtyard.

Above **This is a modern interpretation of a yurt, the traditional shelter of Mongolian nomads. The building sits in the lower pasture, a short distance from the central compound. Adapted from a kit, the yurt provides additional space for visiting family and friends. The entry porch creates a sense of transition from outside to inside and a buffer from the elements.**

Opposite **Inside the yurt, the dome skylight and translucent canvas roof fill the space with soft light, creating a uniquely enjoyable retreat for guests.**

J ane and Doug loved raising their family in a place of such unsurpassed beauty—a secluded meadow atop a towering bluff, all with a panoramic view of an ocean bay and snow-capped mountains. But unlike the perfect setting, the small, basic 1957 ranch-style house they lived in there had always been less than ideal—and it was fast becoming downright inadequate. The couple had no desire to pack up and leave, but as their three children approached their teenage years, something had to be done before the house burst apart at the seams. After years of planning, drawing sketches together around the dinner table, writing up

Bungalow by the Bay

wish lists, and envisioning the home of their dreams, Jane and Doug eventually realized that, for what they really wanted, it would be easier to start over from scratch.

They brought their ideas to architects Richard Hiner and Chris Carson, who drew up plans in which the old house was to be torn down and a new house erected on the old foundation. Reusing the foundation provided the homeowners with all the obvious time- and cost-saving advantages. But while the footprint of their new home was predetermined, nothing about it would be like the old rambler. The house they envisioned was to have the simple lines and broad porches of the shingled Craftsman Bungalow style. Jane and Doug wanted open, spacious public rooms where the family could be together, a separate rec room where the kids could gather with their friends, a special activities room that would be just for the family, ample closets and storage, lots of windows to take in the incomparable view, and private spaces for everyone.

Above *A classic porch entry-way affords the visitor a dramatic view of the bay. Columns set in stone bases and sturdy railings show off the home's solid construction and fine craftsmanship.*

Right *The broad, low-pitched roof, wide dormer, and square windows recall the Craftsman-era homes of the owners' Midwest origins. The broad porches provide covered outdoor space, a much appreciated feature in the rainy Pacific Northwest.*

Left **The west-facing porch overlooks sunsets on the bay, a favorite retreat after a long day at work. One of the first requests the owners made of the architects was for just such a spot to take in the scenery.**

Below **A low partition wall separates the living room from the dining room, while a broad doorway connects the kitchen to the larger space. Pocket doors slide shut to close off the music room without shutting out its light or its sense of connection to the rest of the house. There's no TV in the living room—or anywhere else on this level.**

The Right Balance

Finding the right balance between public and private areas is important in the design of any home. When there are older children and teenagers to consider, the question of the right mix of spaces takes on a special urgency. Whereas young children need to be near parents to feel safe and secure, older children—especially teenagers—need rooms where they can feel independent; because if they can't find what they need at home, they go elsewhere.

Rather than placing the children in a separate bedroom wing as some families do, the homeowners chose to keep all family bedrooms together on the second floor. Doug and Jane dedicated much of the lower level of their new house to a semi-autonomous, acoustically isolated living space for the kids. Easily monitored by parents on the main floor above, the rec room has its own kitchenette and a regulation-size pool table, and it opens onto a basketball court just outside. Not surprisingly, the house is a favorite hangout for the children and their friends. The kids appreciate the high degree of independence they enjoy in the basement retreat and, perhaps, the unconscious security of knowing that the parents are just up the stairs.

In contrast to the secluded rec room on the lower level, the main floor features a living room, dining room, and kitchen that all open onto each other. This is the heart of the home, a generous space for spending time together as a family and preparing and sharing meals near the warmth of the hearth. "This is where we all like to hang out," reports Doug. Expansive windows fill the area with light and look out across the covered porch to the water and mountains. A separate study takes in the view, as well. In addition to accommodating overnight guests, the study provides Doug with a place to do a little work at home without being too isolated from family activities.

Above **On the lower level, a TV and "rowdy room" is designed so that the children and their friends can hang out with some sense of autonomy. A pantry is outfitted with a microwave and a small fridge to keep hungry kids at bay, reducing trips upstairs to the kitchen. The glass-block wall lets in soft natural light while separating the TV area from an adjoining play area.**

Doug and Jane wanted the children to have a hand in the design process, especially in their own rooms, so each bedroom sports features specially requested by the occupant. One son has a "secret" room, a carpeted second closet that is his private domain. Their daughter has a mirrored vanity and sink in her bedroom, a feature that keeps morning bathroom skirmishes between sister and brothers to a minimum.

The most private, most family-oriented space that everyone shares is the third-floor family room. Completely out of the traffic flow of the house, this is a place for homework, computer games, model building, and sewing projects. There is a small, sunny sitting deck just outside the family room, a special perch at the top of the house called the Crow's Nest. The stairway back down to the second floor brings additional light into the core of the house.

A Place for Everything and Everything in its Place

Providing adequate storage—and judiciously located storage—helps families to manage the accumulated "stuff" of modern living. Jane and Doug were very conscious of their storage needs after living for so many years in the tight quarters of their old rambler. Closets are numerous and spacious. Additional built-in storage keeps less frequently used items like sports equipment, camping gear, and seasonal clothing well organized, easy to find, and out of the way.

A spacious, well-lit laundry room has plentiful shelf and counter space and a separate laundry basket for each member of the family. The laundry room is on the second floor, a location that Jane specifically requested so that it would be close to the bedrooms and family bathrooms where most of the laundry is generated.

The kitchen and pantry were carefully designed with the family in mind, as well. Safe placement of appliances and ample counter space make the kitchen a wonderful place for multiple cooks. The

Above **This built-in sink and vanity are tucked under the stairs to the third floor. Although the teenage daughter lobbied for a private bathroom, the compromise of the bedroom sink allows for the privacy she required from younger brothers.**

Opposite **This family project room is at the top of the house, completely out of the traffic flow. There are stations for sewing, hobby projects, and the computer. High windows along the east wall bring in ample natural light, while a center stairwell funnels light down to the bedroom hallway below.**

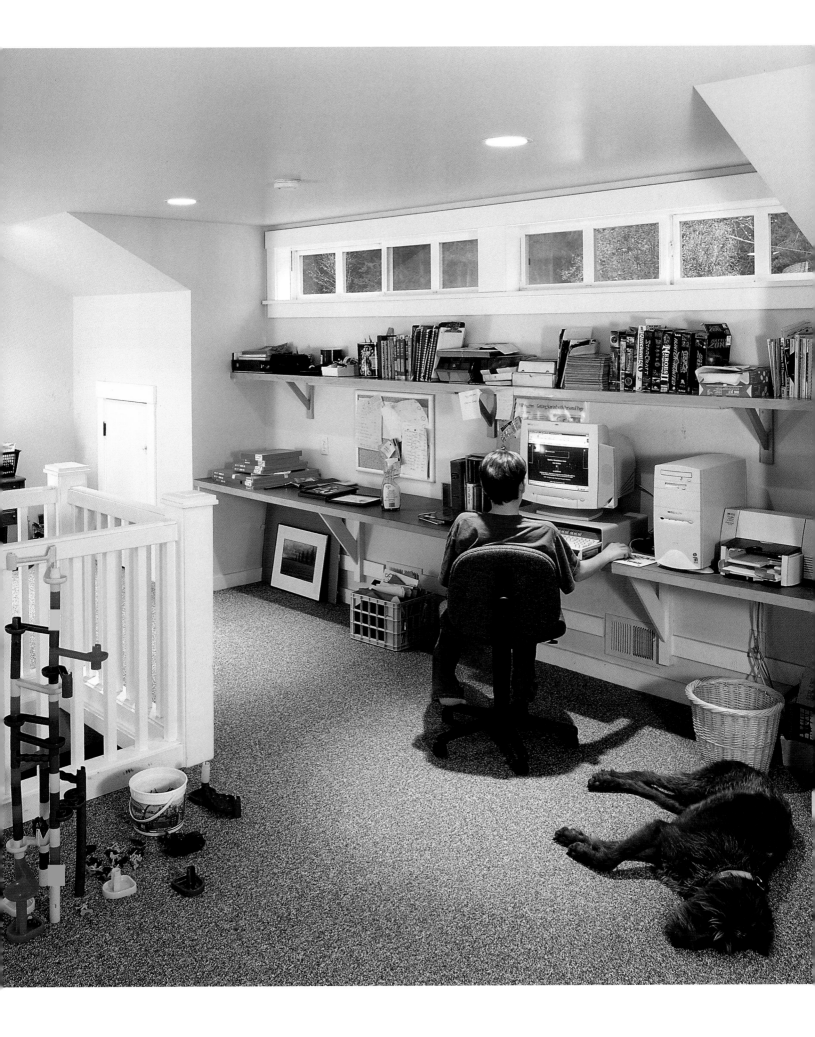

adjacent pantry provides extra storage for staples, which helps the family cut down on trips to the grocery store.

Jane and Doug love their new home as much as they have always loved their beautiful property. They believe that the long process of envisioning and refining their dreams for their new house helped them to grow as a family. They're very clear about one thing—this home helps them live the kind of family life they want for themselves and for their children.

Top left **The kitchen island is a great place for homework and a snack. The thoughtful placement of appliances (notice, for example, that the microwave is placed at counter height) allows kids to participate safely in meal preparation. A kitchen mini-office and cookbook library is set in a niche and keeps household paperwork orga-nized and close at hand.**

Bottom left **A large, pull-out spice rack is positioned opposite the range for easy access. The broad window above the sink brings the water view into the kitchen.**

Bottom right **The large pantry is furnished with built-in shelves, recycling bins, and a broom closet. Dubbed "the Costco room," there's ample storage space for staples— almost a mini-grocery store. The counter surface serves as backup prep space when the family works together creating large meals for company.**

Main Floor

1. Entry
2. Living Room
3. Music Room
4. Kitchen
5. Dining Room
6. Study
7. Utility Room

2nd Floor

8. Bedroom
9. Master Bedroom
10. Master Bath
11. Bathroom
12. Laundry

Attic

13. Family Room

fantasy house

In the words of the mother of this family, "Planning the house was a family occupation, and Doug and I were always interested in what our children had to say. On the other hand, the kids were still young enough to have some major fantasies about what they could have. There was the giant, indoor swimming pool idea; the kids thought that would be really great!"

If Mom and Dad had only been a little more cooperative, the kids would today be living in a home with massive, Southern-plantation-style columns on all four sides. There would be steel cables for gliding directly from bedroom windows to a massive tree fort. Everyone would have their very own suite of rooms, and the family of five would have seven bathrooms.

Secret passageways would lurk behind hidden panels for quick escapes. Instead of a stairway down from the third-floor crow's nest, there would be a fire pole. And, of course, there would be a special TV room with a theater-size screen and surround sound. "I can't remember what all else," laughs Jane, "but they certainly had their opinions."

After years of living in the San Francisco Bay area, Harriet and Russ De Wolfe wanted a quieter community and a more relaxed pace of life for their retirement years. "We wanted a real grandma and grandpa kind of place," explains Harriet. They already owned the perfect piece of property: four wooded acres overlooking the shipping lanes of Puget Sound, just to the north of Seattle. It was just the spot for an old-fashioned farmhouse, for fruit trees and a vegetable garden, for a broad deck to take in the view.

A Scandinavian Farmhouse
in the Pacific Northwest

The home they envisioned was to be comfortable and informal, with a big country kitchen for Harriet, a gourmet cook, and a separate workshop for Russ, a serious hobbyist. It was to have a first-floor master bedroom for them and a pair of cozy second-floor rooms for visits from their grandchildren, family, and friends. Most of all, it was to be a place where no room was off-limits, and everyone felt truly welcome.

Harriet and Russ had traveled extensively in Scandinavia, staying as often as they could in quaint travelers' inns and lodges, many of them old country log structures. Not only would a traditional Scandinavian design honor their family roots, but the style would be especially well suited to the Pacific Northwest coast. They brought their project to Jean Steinbrecher, a northwest architect well known for her log homes and lodges. As the project began to take shape, the De Wolfes realized that the cost of log construction would be prohibitive, but Jean assured them

Above **Rich architectural details and bold colors reinforce this home's ties to its Scandinavian roots. The dragon on the peak (a gift from the contractor) is an ancient Norse symbol.**

Right **When upstairs guest rooms are not occupied, the owners use the space as their private offices. The arched openings, heavy construction, and grooved boards of the built-in bed draw on Scandinavian detailing.**

they could still have all the charm of an old-fashioned Scandinavian family home.

Jean designed a reinterpretation of a Scandinavian farmhouse with traditional board-and-batten siding over a standard frame and heavy, oversize trim elements. Where the old-world original would have had a steeply pitched roof and gabled dormers to deal with winter snowfall, the De Wolfe house features the broad over-hangs and shed-style dormers better suited to the damp, mild Pacific Northwest climate. "It looks as if it had been built here by Scandinavian immigrants," explains Jean.

Front-Row Seat at a Country Kitchen

The center of the home is an ample country kitchen, the largest space in the house. A broad butcher-block countertop, featuring a second kitchen sink, separates this serious cook's kitchen from the home's only dining area on the other side of the room. Built-in banquette seating lines the walls around an antique Danish dining table that can expand to seat 20.

The trend toward a more informal style of living is evident in the De Wolfe home, and it is important to note how much home-owners and guests alike enjoy this comfortable approach to enter-taining. According to Russ, when guests arrive here for a dinner party, they make themselves right at home in the kitchen and are usually still sitting around the dining table at the end of the evening. Not only do family and friends appreciate having a front-row seat to the action in the kitchen, but Harriet and Russ never feel isolated from the fun at their own parties.

Even when it is just the two of them, the kitchen/dining area is the most used room in the house, the place where Russ and Harriet tend to hang out during the day. It opens onto the living room, a cozy gathering space that features a view out to the water,

Opposite, top **Relatively small and cozy, the living room is open to the kitchen and dining room through an expansive open passageway. Built-in bookshelves in the living room mirror the book-shelves just inside the doorway to the kitchen.**

Opposite, bottom **The bright, well-lit kitchen opens to the dining area. The hanging rack puts pots and pans conveniently close at hand while creating a visual sepa-ration between work space and sitting area. The wood floors and countertops are a mellow contrast to the white cupboards and yellow walls.**

the mountains, and the sunset. Russ keeps a set of powerful binoculars mounted on a tripod at the living room window so he can keep track of the boat traffic in the shipping lanes just off-shore. Typically, the living room is the place where the De Wolfes come to unwind at the end of the day. "Every time you look out the windows here, you're on vacation," comments Harriet. The rooms are painted a rich yellow and trimmed in bright white. One of 17 traditional Scandinavian colors that have been used throughout the house, it's a sunny look that warms the space on even the rainiest day.

Places to be Together, Rooms to Be Apart

From the moment they started thinking about this retirement home, the De Wolfes knew that it would be the place where they would live out their lives together. They enjoy many common activities and pastimes, from environmental volunteer work to their gourmet club. But they are realists, too, so they asked Jean to give them lots of spaces where they could spread out and be apart from each other. On any given day, Harriet is likely to be cooking up something in the kitchen while Russ is at work out in his shop.

The two upstairs guest bedrooms are often full of visiting family and friends, but they serve double duty as study/offices for Russ and Harriet as well. A third upstairs room was an unexpected bonus. During construction, the De Wolfes had planned to leave this attic space unfinished, but when a contractor accidentally installed drywall, Russ and Harriet saw what a charming little room it was. It has turned out to be especially useful, too. "Russ loves watching professional boxing, and I don't," explains Harriet with a laugh. "So he watches his boxing on the TV in the little upstairs den."

Above **Part of the detached garage, the shop is just steps away from the house. The magnificent 19th-century pot-belly stove was restored and rebuilt by the homeowner.**

Opposite **Tucked into a stand of towering fir trees, the house blends traditional forms, rich colors, and bold detailing to convey the impression of an old-time European farmhouse.**

Below **The Scandinavian-style beds feature built-in reading lamps, bookshelves, and under-bed storage drawers.**

When the owners of this house resolved to move their family to the coast of Maine, the decision was based in large part on the quality of life they wanted to provide for their children. Both husband and wife had grown up in rural, seaside settings, and they wanted their children to have woods to hike in, fields to play in, and tide pools to explore. The land they found met all of their requirements: it was on the waterfront, it was covered with beautiful, tall trees, it was near a good town with good schools, and it was very private. The property featured a sunny knoll right by the shoreline—the perfect site on which to build their family home—but a

The Maine House

pair of deep ravines and problematic access posed very real concerns. Before spending their money, they felt it would be wise to consult with a local architect.

One Step at a Time

They brought their concerns to Portland architect Rob Whitten. After careful study of the site, Rob was able to assure the couple that with careful planning they could definitely build their family home on the sunny knoll. The couple next asked Rob to design a small, interim cottage for them. They wanted to get the cottage up as quickly and efficiently as possible so that they and their children could begin living on the property right away. Later on, when their family home was built, the cottage would become their guest house. The 1,400-sq.-ft. cottage was designed and erected in less than four months. The family moved in, the children were enrolled in the local schools, and the real planning began.

The couple wanted their new home to complement the property. It was to feature rustic—but not too rustic—styling, a variety of

Above **The chalet-style second-floor balcony expands a child's small bedroom right into the trees. The balustrade of peeled branches is a typical northern New England camp design element.**

Right **Exposed timber trusses, wood paneling, and a dramatically painted gable ceiling define the living room as a space apart from the more casual family room. The large picture windows are bisected with sashwork to reinforce the traditional camp-cottage style and to frame the expansive views.**

table to create an intimate pool of light after the sun sets. Richly upholstered dining chairs help make the dining area an especially comfortable place for the family to gather.

Getting Away from It All

As much as this family enjoys spending time together, the house provides a variety of useful, comfortable spaces to be apart. The living room is a wonderful place to gather with guests, but it also sees much use as a place for family members to get away from it all, practice the piano, and enjoy the front-row view of the shoreline. During the summer months, the windows here can be opened, creating a porchlike feeling as the living room fills with the sea breeze.

A first-floor bedroom is a part-time guest room, but it is used primarily as a professional home office. According to the homeowners, the room is placed far enough away from the kitchen/family room to allow for a feeling of separation from family activities. At the same time, the home office is really just off the main child traffic pattern through the house, near mudroom, bathroom, and stairs, so a parent working here can easily keep tabs on the kids.

Family bedrooms are clustered on the second floor. The entrance to the master bedroom is through a short, private hallway, which helps to establish it as a space apart. The children's bedrooms each have two ample closets, a design strategy that puts an end to the question of where to put all the stuff. While the children's bedrooms are not especially large, there is more than ample storage space for clothes, toys, and sports equipment.

The homeowners feel that Rob really listened to them, and as a result their home is everything they wanted it to be. There are no unused spaces here, no formal rooms gathering dust. Rather, it is a warm, relaxed family home—and a true expression of the people who live there.

Above *Originally planned as a dead-space storage area, a flash of inspiration and a dash of red paint transformed this room into a special kid retreat. The tiny window brings in natural light, and thick-pile carpets and bean-bag furniture create a space where any child would love to play house—or video games, or Legos, or have sleepovers.*

Opposite *The cathedral ceiling and exposed trusses add visual interest to the master bedroom, as well as a sense of spaciousness. French doors lead to a small, private deck with views of the trees and the water beyond.*

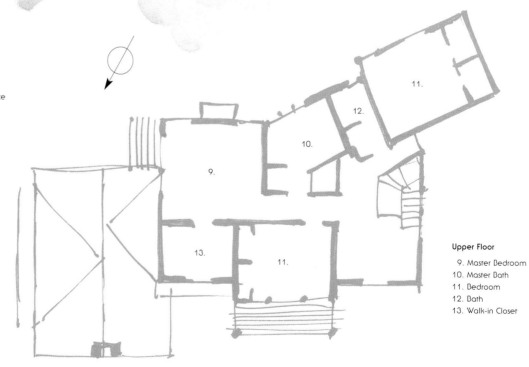

Main Floor

1. Entry
2. Dining Room
3. Kitchen
4. Living Room
5. Family Room
6. Guest Room/Office
7. Bath
8. Mudroom

Upper Floor

9. Master Bedroom
10. Master Bath
11. Bedroom
12. Bath
13. Walk-in Closet

room at the top

An extra-large landing at the top of the stairs was originally planned as homework central, a place where the two children in this family would have their desks, a computer, and bookshelves. In fact, compact, built-in bookshelves here make excellent use of eave space that might otherwise go to waste, but there isn't a desk or a computer in sight. Instead, a cozy love seat fills the niche between the bookshelves.

This is a mini-family room, a special space set away from the busy comings and goings of the household. According to the homeowners, the mini-family room tends to be used late in the day. While kids are washing up and getting in their pj's, Mom or Dad might be here on the landing folding a basket of laundry. Before lights out, there's always time to cuddle up on the love seat for a bedtime story and a kiss goodnight.

Above **The jogged footprint brings the view into every region of the house. A generously sized bay window, sheltered under the roof overhang, expands the living room and draws in the outdoors.**

Architects and Designers

A Bungalow Built for Change (pp. 20-27)
Johan and Robin Luchsinger (Bayliss Brand Wagner Architects),
10801 Main Street, Bellevue, WA 98004; (425) 454-0566

A Garden Home in the Heart of the City (pp. 28-35)
Bobby-Sue Hood (Hood-Miller Associates), 60 Federal Street,
Suite 401, San Fransisco, CA 94107-1430; (415) 777-5775

Texas Family Farmhouse (pp. 36-43)
Ken Foster, 272 Washington Street, Camden, ME 04843;
(207) 236-0224

At Home in the Minnesota Pines (pp. 44-51)
Katherine Cartrette, 904 South 4th Street, Stillwater, MN 55082;
(651) 351-0961

Starting Small, Dreaming Big (pp. 52-57)
Gene and Chris Callahan (Black Oak General Contracting),
172 Puddleby Lane, Fieldbrook, CA 95521; (707) 839-3329

Home for the Weekend (pp. 58-67)
Ernest and Grace Gordon Collins, 200-312 East Esplanade, North
Vancouver, British Columbia, Canada V7L 1A4; (604) 983-3125

By the Beautiful Sea (pp. 68-75)
Andy Neumann, 888 Linden Avenue, Carpenteria, CA 93013;
(805) 684-8885

Family Dream Home (pp. 76-85)
Peter Breese, PO Box 2726, Vineyard Haven, MA 02568;
(508) 693-8272

A Home for the Generations (pp. 86-93)
Virginia Dawson Lane, 10 Gillon Street, Charleston, SC 29401;
(843) 853-4126

At Home on the Hill (pp. 94-101)
Sheldon Pennoyer and David O'Neil (Pennoyer-O'Neil Architects),
661 Massachusetts Avenue, Arlington, MA 02476; (718) 648-7420

Timeless Beauty for a Modern Family (pp. 102-109)
Fu Tung Cheng, 2808 San Pablo Avenue, Berkeley, CA 94702;
(510) 849-3272

Life on the River (pp. 110-117)
Michaela Mahady and Dan Porter, 904 South 4th Street,
Stillwater, MN 55082; (651) 351-0961

At Play in Santa Barbara (pp. 118-125)
Brian and Judi Cearnal, 521½ State Street, Santa Barbara,
CA 93101; (805) 963-8077

Northwoods Formal (pp. 126-133)
Robert Gerloff, 4007 Sheridan Avenue South, Minneapolis,
MN 55410; (612) 927-5913

Full Bloom in the Desert (pp. 134-141)
John Anderson, 912 Roma Avenue NW, Albuquerque, NM 87102;
(505) 764-8306

A Tale of Two Families (pp. 142-149)
Mac Godley, Box 190, Hadlyme, CT 06439; (860) 434-9262

Fly Away Home (pp. 150-157)
Andrew Reese/Ray Weber, Port Townsend, WA 98368;
(360) 385-4305

The Many Lives of a Four-Flat (pp. 158-165)
Scott Rappe (Kuklinski + Rappe Architects), 1915 West Division
Street, Chicago, IL 60622; (773) 276-5700

The New Family Farmhouse (pp. 166-173)
Andy Neumann, 888 Linden Avenue, Carpenteria, CA 93013;
(805) 684-8885

The Weekend Family Home (pp. 174-181)
Jeremiah Eck, 81 Canal Street, Boston, MA 02114; (617) 367-9696

Blue Heron Ranch (pp. 182-189)
Enrico and Nadia Natali, PO Box 1318, Ojai, CA 93024;
(805) 646-4404

Bungalow by the Bay (pp. 190-197)
Christopher Carson and Richard Hiner (Hiner-Carson Architects),
1008 Lawrence Street, Port Townsend, WA 98368; (360) 385-3262

**A Scandinavian Farmhouse in the Pacific Northwest
(pp. 198-205)**
Jean Steinbrecher, PO Box 788, Langley, WA 98260; (360) 221-0494

The Maine House (pp. 206-213)
Rob Whitten (with Will Winkleman), 37 Silver Steet, Portland,
ME 04112; (207) 774-0111